The
FOCUS
FULFILLED
Life

Ed Turose

The FOCUS FULFILLED *Life*

PUBLISHED BY PALM TREE PUBLICATIONS
A DIVISION OF PALM TREE PRODUCTIONS
KELLER, TEXAS U.S.A.
PRINTED IN THE U.S.A.

www.palmtreeproductions.net

Palm Tree Productions is a Media Services Company dedicated to seeing the Kingdom of God advanced by ministries and businesses with excellence, integrity and professionalism through the use of high quality media resources. Whether the publication is print, audio or visual, we are dedicated to excellence in every aspect from concept to final production.

It is our desire that this publication will enrich your life and cause you to increase in wisdom and understanding.

For more information about products and services available through Palm Tree Productions, visit our website at www.palmtreeproductions.net.

THE FOCUS FULFILLED LIFE
© Copyright 2007 by Ed Turose

Cover Photos: Big Stock Photos, The Big Box of Art 1,000,000,000

ISBN: 978-0979-54805-5

To contact the author, visit
www.edturose.com

TABLE OF CONTENTS

The FOCUS FULFILLED *Life*

ACKNOWLEDGEMENTS

"Focus is what is required by men and women who are the best at whatever they do! Tiger Woods must be focused to win so many championships. Nascar drivers must be focused to drive at 200 m.p.h. and win. Double mindedness is a plague in the church today. People are living in the land of almost. This is the reason this book has come for such a time as this. Our spiritual, social, relational, physical and financial life must be a daily exercise of fruitful focus. There's a pub in Ireland that sits on a bluff off the Atlantic Ocean. It has a sign out front that says "Ireland's Most Fantastic View, Fog Permitting." Surprisingly, they have a high sale of post cards. We know the view in life is awesome, we just need the fog to clear so we can see what our faith says is already there. Focus is that great tool to clear the fog of life away so we can clearly see what God has for each of us! Good job, Ed, stay focused — we need to see things clearly!"

- Bishop Bart Pierce
Rock City Church, Baltimore, MD

"Ed Turose is an effective Christian corporate leader, business and wealth building instructor, consultant, mentor, and motivational speaker who has written a power packed impartation about your need to focus.

A lack of focus is why many people fail. Your focus determines your destiny. *The Focus Fulfilled Life* brings clarity, guidance, and help for you to succeed. To those who receive an understanding of focus, the power of focus will help you succeed and achieve greater things! You need *The Focus Fulfilled Life*."

- John P. Kelly, CEO
International Christian WealthBuilders Foundation

Chapter One

The POWER of FOCUS

Results, Achievements and Success

What would life be like if you could stay focused on a goal or objective and see greater results? Because I have focused, here are just a few results I have achieved in my life: three Little League Championships, a four year starting position on a small college football team, graduation from college with a BSBA degree, successful management results through people in two Fortune 500 companies and two time recipient of the Salesman of the Year award. All these objectives were reached because I focused on specific areas in order to reap this success.

The world's system is corrupted by a 'produce mentality.' This obsession causes stress, anxiety, pressure and oppression. <u>But God's system is a system of seedtime and harvest, or sowing and reaping.</u> God's system allows for a natural rhythm of work and rest that is filled with faith and hope, free from stress, filled with provision, and designed for victory. In this book, *The Focus Fulfilled Life*, I will show you how to create a process for a focused lifestyle by

God's System

utilizing the Word of God and activating your faith, in order
to see a harvest. Through the power of a focused fulfilled
lifestyle, you can obtain a manifestation of the promises
you are believing for.

The Amplified Bible says in Matthew 6:33, "But seek
(aim at and strive for or focus on) first of all His kingdom
and His righteousness (His way of doing and being right)
and then all these things, will be given to you besides."
The word focus means to meditate or to consider. Below
I have summarized the definitions of the words focus and
meditate.

☞ FOCUS

- directed attention (attend – to apply
  one's self, to apply the mind) "My son,
  attend to my words; incline thine ear
  unto my sayings." Proverbs 4:20 (KJV)

- a point of concentration; "My son, attend
  unto My wisdom, and bow thy ear to My
  understanding." Proverbs 5:1 (KJV)

☞ MEDITATE

- to engage in mental exercise for the
  purpose of reaching a heightened
  level of spiritual awareness;

- to plan or project in the mind; however, the
  Hebrews considered that to meditate upon
  the Scriptures is to quietly repeat them in a
  soft droning sound, while utterly abandoning
  outside distractions. From this tradition comes
  a specialized type of Jewish prayer called
  "davening," that is, reciting texts, praying
  intense prayers, or getting lost in communion

with God while bowing or rocking back and forth. Evidently this dynamic form of meditation-prayer (focus) goes all the way back to David's time. *(Spirit Life Bible Word Wealth, page 753.)*

In other words, when you begin to meditate or focus on specific areas, you will receive a manifestation which will produce multiplication. Let's review a few examples from the Bible.

> "This Book of the Law shall not depart out of your mouth, but you shall meditate on it day and night, that you may observe and do according to all that is written in it. For then you shall make your way prosperous, and then you shall deal wisely and have good success." Joshua 1:8 AMP

Do you want to have good success in your life?

> "And Isaac went out to meditate in the field and lifted up his eyes and looked, and there, the camels were coming. They were bringing his future bride. He meditated before God and God brought him his wife!" Genesis 24:63 (SFLB)

> "When I remember You on my bed, I meditate on You in the night watches. This is the place where I have spent many hours by meditating and focusing on God's Word on my bed and listen to hear the voice of the Holy Spirit behind God's Word." Psalm 63:6 (SFLB)

Psalm 119:15, 23, 48, 78, and 145 all speak about a person meditating on God's Word, His statutes, and His precepts.

Meditate on the Word

Psalm 143:5 tells us that we need to daily meditate on the works of God and thank Him for all He has done for us!

> "Meditate on these things (be an example in word, conversation, in charity, in spirit, in faith, in purity, neglect not the gift God has given you) so people can see how you profited in doing it!"
> 1 Timothy 4:9-15 AMP

Psalm 34:10 tells us that they that seek or focus on (inquire and require) the Lord (by right of their need and on the authority of His Word), and that because of this none of them shall lack any beneficial thing.

God is a God of manifestation. In other words, you have the evidence of seeing results that can be measured. Many people I know have not yet reaped a harvest. They have sowed but they have not reaped.

Why do we sow without reaping? I believe it is because we do not focus long enough (by using the Word) on the area we want to see changed. God wants to bless you and He stands at the door and knocks and He will come to you when you open the door of your heart and begin to focus on Him. James 4:8 *KJV* says, "Draw nigh to God and He will draw nigh to you."

God is a God of Increase Unto Multiplication

> "And God said to them, 'Be fruitful and multiply, and fill the earth and subdue it (using all its vast resources in the service of God and man) and have dominion.'"
> Genesis 1:28 AMP

The word multiply means to increase in number — especially greatly or in multiples. We need to become people of multiplication, which is a process of continual increase. How are we going to do this? We will begin to see multiplication when we start to focus on specific manifestations in the next 40 days.

> "Blessed (happy, fortunate, prosperous, and enviable) is the man who walks and lives not in the counsel of the ungodly (following their advice, their plans and purposes), nor stands (submissive and inactive) in the path where sinners walk, nor sits down (to relax and rest) where the scornful (and the mockers) gather. But his delight and desire are in the law of the Lord, and on His law (the precepts, the instructions, the teachings of God) he habitually meditates (ponders and studies) by day and by night."   Psalm 1:1-2 AMP.

God has a system — a system of sowing and reaping or seedtime and harvest. When we meditate (or focus) on His Word and apply that Word into many different situations of our life (situations that affect our spirit, our soul, our body, our social or financial realms), this is our seed. The results of planting seeds of focus (on God's Word and the application of His Word) will bring greater success in the areas of our lives. These results are our harvest.

Prototypes

Jesus and John the Baptist were both prototypes of the power of focusing. They were successful because they responded to their call, to complete their work on planet earth. Let's take a look at Luke, chapter one. We see a specific Scripture that most people never look at and it is about the life of John the Baptist. Luke 1:80 *AMP* says, "And the little boy (John the Baptist) grew and became strong in spirit; and he was in the deserts (wilderness) until the day of his appearing to Israel (the commencement of his public ministry).

Here is a prototype of a focused life on planet earth. By looking at John the Baptist, we see that when somebody focuses on what their assignment is, they will be successful. They will fulfill their purpose and reach their destiny. John was chosen to be the forerunner for Jesus. It was his assignment to prepare the way for the coming of the Lord. He focused on that call and saw great success.

A little later in Luke, we read a verse about Jesus during His childhood. "And the Child grew and became strong in spirit, filled with wisdom; and the grace (favor and spiritual blessing) of God was upon Him" Luke 2:40 *AMP*. Even as a child, Jesus applied Himself to knowing the Father's will and focused on His purpose.

Both Jesus and John were prototypes who focused on the specific work that they were destined to do on planet earth. Both had tremendous results. Jesus, obviously, is our prototype for life. Jesus knew His purpose and was focused on fulfilling His destiny. Even in His deity and with perfect faith and fellowship with the Father, Jesus still faced temptation and distraction. What makes us think that we will not face distractions that will hinder our focus and keep us from achieving our destiny? We MUST learn how to focus. Not only must we learn HOW to focus, but we must also learn WHAT to focus on and HOW TO APPLY this to our daily life. Only then will we see true breakthrough and experience lasting victory!

This book will reveal some of these hindrances to you. You must understand that as you begin to focus on specific aspects of your life, there's going to be a battle. Every time that I have taken a step toward spiritual increase in my life, I have always faced opposition – and his name is Satan. The Bible clearly tells us in John 10:10 that he (Satan) comes to steal, to kill and to destroy. He understands that if you focus on God's Word and apply it to your life carefully and purposefully with a clear goal – you WILL be successful. You WILL have victory. He does

NOT want this to happen! In this same verse, John 10:10, we see the tremendous plan of God when Jesus says, "I have come to give you life and that life more abundantly." This is God's plan for you – abundant life. If your life is not filled with spiritual wealth, emotional balance, physical wholeness, relational completeness, and financial abundance, then you have room for God to work in you! You have a need to FOCUS.

The Kingdom of God is focused on His system of seedtime and harvest (Mark 4). We know that we are supposed to sow the Word of God into every situation we have in order to get tremendous and greater results. We also know that as we begin to do this, there is going to be a conflict, a battle. Distractions, anxiety and temptation too often block us from our focused pursuit and steal our victory.

> "Then the cares and anxieties of the world and distractions of the age, and the pleasure and delight and false glamour and deceitfulness of riches, and the craving and passionate desire for other things creep in and choke and suffocate the Word, and it becomes fruitless." Mark 4:19 AMP

I don't want to deal with what keeps you from success. I want to deal with what causes you to gain success! The ministry that my wife and I have, Ministers of Kingdom Finance, is focused on taking you to the next level. You go to the next level by practical application of the Word of God in your life. For over thirty years I have worked in Fortune 500 companies. In this arena, I have helped individuals focus on achieving goals and objectives and they have had great success time and time again. Recently, I was with the vice president of a major Fortune 500 company I work for in the juice and drink business. He told me that I was the number one practitioner in the country and he asked me how I did it. What I am about to share with you is the key to repeatable success. I am going to give you what you need in order for you to take a practical step in developing a lifestyle of focusing on goals and objectives.

Got Goals?

Studies show that a mere 3% of the population sets goals. That means that 97% of individuals on the earth do not have a focus mentality and do not create objectives. They go through life meeting the expectations given to them by others. Even worse, they go through life living day-to-day, paycheck to paycheck, social encounter to social encounter without any real purpose or sense of contributing to something greater than they are or having a valuable impact in the lives of others.

There was a study done back in the 1950's at a major university in the east. What they did was to look at the senior graduation class of that particular year. Through a survey, they divided them up into groups of individuals who set goals and individuals who did not set goals. Thirty years later, they gathered these individuals together. They noticed that those who set goals (thirty years prior) were more productive, had more financial provision, had a greater spiritual focus in their life and had a better relationship with individuals they dealt with — all based on the goals they set. Those who did not set goals were 'behind' in almost every area of life including jobs, earning potential, successful relationships, health, etc. So, setting goals and objectives and developing strategies to reach those goals and objectives really does work.

Study proved it!

Jesus had a Plan

<u>Jesus had a plan to take the earth</u>. Jesus had a plan of action. How was he able to get the Gospel throughout the whole earth with only twelve individuals? He had these individuals focus on taking the Gospel throughout the world. He sent out 70 individuals to go into cities and spread the Gospel. The Bible tells us he had advance teams that went out to preach the Word of God.

Focused for Healing

Let me tell you how critical it is to have a focused mentality in your life and to create a lifestyle of focus. I have a few examples that I want to share with you that are very powerful in terms of getting individuals focused. Let me share about my best friend, Jim Sanderbeck. Jim and I have a covenant relationship with each other, that means his friends are my friends, his enemies are my enemies, my resources are his resources and I am committed to his success just as he is committed to mine. The testimony I am about to share is one of life and death.

During the summer of 2005, Pastor Jim Sanderbeck unexpectedly died from a heart attack brought about by Lyme disease. Upon arrival at the emergency room and undergoing a heart catheterization, medical personnel declared that he was in the midst of a massive heart attack and in a condition called heart block (i.e. the receiving and pumping chambers could not electrically communicate with each other). Later, as determined by an echocardiogram, two walls of his heart were extensively damaged, and one valve was leaking over three (on a four point scale). The next day his deteriorating condition manifested in ventricular fibrillation and he suffered cardiac arrest. When Cindy and I received the word that Jim went into cardiac arrest, Cindy and I immediately fell on our faces declaring life over his physical body. I then heard the inner voice say to me "I stopped it, get up and begin to praise Me for he will live and not die". I then received a call within 30 seconds after we began to thank God telling me they were able to revive Jim and bring him back. Because my wife and I have spent time <u>focusing</u> on hearing the voice of God, we were able to stand and begin to praise God for the answer He spoke to us! Clinically dead for over seven minutes, he was greeted in heaven by three angels, saw the entrance to hell and walked in the courtyards of heaven. After those seven minutes, he was resuscitated; flown by emergency helicopter to another hospital, and entered into a week long *focused* battle for life.

My wife, Cindy, and I had walked in covenant love with Jim and his wife, Esther, for many years. This covenant relationship allowed us to grow in uncompromising faith through study of the Word of God, and by spending time in the presence of the Father. The fruit of this relationship had prepared Jim, his family and his closest friends for this incredible battle. For the entire 7-day battle, operational covenant love was expressed in an unending *focus* of prayer, reading and declaration of the Word of God, and worship. At night, I would walk under the open sky, crying out to God and demanding Satan to release his grip on Jim's life. Hundreds prayed and requested prayer from other believers around the world while the Sanderbeck family courageously witnessed to the hospital staff, worshiped God, and did spiritual warfare for Jim's healing.

On the sixth night, Jesus came by the Spirit into the hospital ICU and spoke to Jim. Their intimate communion, coupled with Jesus' personal instruction, culminated as Jesus took him through the wall that separates the natural and spiritual realms. In that place of His presence, Jesus revealed the reality, availability and power of covenant love. He showed and taught Pastor Sanderbeck about the

└ Jesus' interaction with Jim

River of God, and the fullness of His manifested power for healing and protection. Jim experienced seven encounters with God that night, separated by approximately two hour intervals. During each of the seven encounters, as Pastor Sanderbeck obeyed Jesus' instruction, his heart rate of 24 beats per minute rose to 72. His blood pressure rose from 72/48 to 120/85.

On the night of July 4th, 2005, Cindy and I spent another time of _focused_ prayer with Jim and Esther. We anointed Jim with oil (according to James 5:15), and supernaturally, Jim's healing was made complete. As we left the hospital in Pittsburgh, PA, we received a phone call about ten minutes into our drive home that something was happening in Jim's body at that time. The results after a few tests that night revealed all extensive damage to the walls of his heart were healed. The damaged valve that was profusely leaking was miraculously repaired without medical intervention and Jim's heart was fully restored. Doctors were at a loss for a medical explanation. That was in 2005. I am writing this book two full years later, and Jim's heart still operates with absolute perfection and all traces of the Lyme disease are gone.

The years of sowing in the Spirit and operating in obedience to remain _focused until victory was fully achieved_ has impacted Jim's life forever. He now travels extensively, proclaiming his testimony, *"Heaven, Hell & Healing: I Came Back to Let You Know It's Real."*[1]

Jim and I both came into agreement to focus on his total wholeness and health. God did a miracle. The reason why God did a miracle begins with the covenant relationship we have with each other that is so strong and so powerful that God's covenant love for us, and our love for each other and our families, manifested itself in Jim's total healing and deliverance.

---

[1]*For speaking engagements or to purchase a copy of his video, please contact Jim Sanderbeck at www.rocksolidas.com or call 724-528-4575.*

Focused for Assignment

I want to share a second testimony about a friend of mine who is a pastor. He told me that he began to focus on setting people free in the area of deliverance. He focused on what the Word of God said about this and began to read other books on the subject and find out what understanding others had gained by their study. (For the next nine months, this friend focused on reading materials, underlining materials, going into the books of the Bible, reading testimonies and focused on how Jesus delivered others, through great men of God, to help people get free from the weaknesses of their flesh.) The result of this period of focus was that the power of God came into his life. He now has an effective ministry of deliverance; setting people free from weaknesses of their flesh.

he did research

Focused for Financial Freedom

Let me give you an example from my own personal life in the area of financial provision. In 1991, I truly wanted to get debt free. I had a mortgage and a few other bills. I focused on this area and was able to gain strategies from the study of some individuals who were teaching on biblical financial principles. I studied this information and began to focus on financial objectives for a period of time. I took the Word of God and began to confess what the Word said about financial provision over my debt. As I began to study the Word of God and began to get revelation knowledge, I focused on getting out of debt. I began by taking one bill, paying that bill off, then taking the money I was using to pay off that bill and apply it to another bill. I began to see my debt reduced somewhat. In 1993, I truly got focused on getting out of debt — and I mean focused! By July of 1993, I was completely debt free — even from my mortgage!

apply the word

16

I believe that God honored my ability to focus for that particular time frame.

Focused for Revelation

In November 1992, a tremendous woman of God came into my church and gave me a word. I want to share that word with you. I knew even then that there was power that came from focusing on God's Word. At that time, in my own personal life, I was focusing on specific Scriptures. My focused meditation was centered on Ephesians 1:17-19.

> For I always pray to the God of our Lord Jesus Christ, the Father of glory, that He may grant you a spirit of wisdom and revelation (of insight into mysteries and secrets) in the (deep and intimate) knowledge of Him, by having the eyes of your heart flooded with light, so that you can know and understand the hope to which He has called you, and how rich is His glorious inheritance in the saints (His set-apart ones), and (so that you can know and understand) what is the immeasurable and unlimited and surpassing greatness of His power in and for us who believe, as demonstrated in the working of His mighty strength,..."
>
> Ephesians 1:17-19 AMP

I was crying out for wisdom and revelation to understand God's Word. I began to take my time and study the Scriptures. I began every day by getting up and confessing these particular verses over my life. I focused on my spiritual growth. As I was doing this, a mighty woman of God named Fuscia Pickett came to my church and called me up and began to speak into my life.

She said, "Son, you have been one that has been saying, 'I want the Teacher to teach me the Book.' You say, 'I want to be able to hear what He said, not what somebody else said.' You have cried out to want to know revelation. Well, I have news for you. My father says that Ephesians, the first chapter, beginning with the seventeenth verse is going to be yours. He is going to grant unto you, not a word of wisdom, not a word of knowledge, but the spirit of wisdom and the spirit of knowledge. The Teacher is on duty. Don't stay out of the classroom. You see, the classroom is inside of you. Go in and read the Bible and have Him (the Teacher) teach it to you. He said that there is open to you a spirit of wisdom, not just a word. The Holy Spirit will move in you in wisdom and knowledge and revelation - and when you stand to preach, it won't be your words, it will be what He taught you."

God was trying to show me that when I began to focus for spiritual growth in my life, He began answering my cry. God confirmed it through the voice of one of His servants to encourage me to remain focused. That was exactly what I needed to hear because I was crying out for the spirit of wisdom and revelation. I wanted this to manifest in my life and was willing to focus, not yield to distraction and see the fullness or wisdom and revelation bearing fruit in my life.

My Promise to You

I want to encourage you that in this book I am going to deal with all aspects of your life. I am going to deal with your spiritual growth. I am going to address your soul, your emotions, your will and your intellect and the weaknesses of your flesh. I'm going to deal with your physical body and your need for wholeness — where there is nothing missing and nothing broken. I am going to deal with your social relationships — that God can bring forth a wholeness in your social relationships with others and with your family, your spouse and your children. I am going to deal with your finances. I know that you need a financial blessing upon your life to live free from debt and to be able to build the kingdom of God by using your resources.

God has anointed me to help others experience a breakout and go to the next level. I have experienced the power of focus in my own life and witnessed this same power in the lives of others. I understand what it takes to set goals and objectives and how to coach you through the process of doing this on your own as well as developing strategies to accomplish your goals. I am committed to helping others succeed by the power of God – to walk in His promises and fulfill their destinies. I am excited to begin this journey with you and pray that as you read, you will begin to apply what you learn and see real results. Come explore your potential with me. The power of focus is in your hands, waiting to be unleashed.

FOCUS Points

A SUMMARY OF WHAT YOU HAVE LEARNED

- ☞ Focusing on and meditating on God's Word will produce success.

- ☞ Only 3% of the population sets goals while 97% need a process for success. *The Focus Fulfilled Life* can help you create a lifestyle of focusing on specific goals and objectives to get better results.

- ☞ God will always do His part as you do yours. As you specifically focus on key areas (such as healing, destiny, finances, social relationships or revelation), God will do His part.

"When I remember Thee
upon my bed, and meditate
on Thee in the night watches.
This is the place where I
have spent many hours by
meditating and focusing
on God's Word on my bed
and listen to hear
the voice of the Holy Spirit
behind God's Word."

Psalm 63:6 (SFLB)

Chapter Two

WHY Do I Need To FOCUS?

Satistics tell us only 3% of the population sets goals. Another statistic, based on the DISC behavioral analysis, suggests that 86% of the population need a process in place in order to be successful. While working for a major Fortune 500 company, I have successfully managed individuals for more than thirty years. My experience has shown me that many people have a personality style that does not set goals. To be successful in causing individuals to reach their potential, I had to create a process for them to set goals and then hold them accountable to the process to achieve those goals.

In *The Focus Fulfilled Life*, I will help you put a process in place for your success. I must stress, however, that accountability to the process is a vital component to your success. I encourage you to have accountability through a pastor or minister, through a small group or with other friends on a weekly basis. Why do you need accountability? Because there are so many distractions around you. Mark 4:19 says that these are the cares and anxieties of the world, distractions of the age, false glamour, deceitfulness of riches, and desires for other things. These distractions

will hinder you from the process and sabotage your discipline. You MUST remain FOCUSED if you are to reach your goals. Accountability helps you do this.

Goals are Vital to Success

Those who set goals and remain focused on those goals achieve greater results than those who have no goals, or, who have unclear goals and lack the focus to follow through with their objectives. Wandering through life, hoping for success, but without even defining what success is, will only leave you frustrated and unfulfilled. Having no goals and not applying yourself with any diligence to study, to training and to the application of knowledge, is a sure formula for small achievement and limited success. **Defining and setting goals is vital to your success in life.** You need goals for every area of your life - spiritual, emotional, relational, physical and financial. **Achieving these goals is dependent upon the process you put in place that allows you to create a strategy, focus on the plan and measure your results.** You CAN be successful in every area of your life. It IS possible to fulfill your destiny and lead a victorious, overcoming, fruitful life that is filled with joy, wholeness and the fruit of the spirit. Many people desire the outcome, but lack the knowledge and ability to achieve it. In *The Focus Fulfilled Life*, I will help you set goals, create a strategy and put a process in place that will help you be successful.

In my own experience, whenever I have focused on key areas of my life, I have seen greater results. Focus sharpens my sword. The Bible says in Ephesians 6:17 that we have a Sword of the Spirit which is the Word of God. We must keep ourselves sharp at all times. We know that the enemy comes to kill, to steal and to destroy (John 10:10). We know that there are situations that come into the workplace, into our social or family life that can cause distraction, suck up large amounts of time and make us lose our focus. When we lose focus, we let down our guard and allow the enemy room to come in. When we lose focus, our sword becomes dull. This makes it difficult to divide between good and evil, better and best, wise and foolish.

I once heard a story that was set in frontier days. Two men were sent into the forest to clear a section of trees. One man, young and strong, set quickly to his task and began cutting. With amazing speed, the trees fell before him and he worked feverishly to cut as many trees as he could. The other man was of smaller physical stature, but with equal determination, began cutting his section of trees. About every forty-five minutes or so, the smaller man disappeared for fifteen minutes, and then returned to continue cutting. The young, strong man would mumble something about being lazy under his breath and continue cutting. As lunch approached, the strong man was ahead and feeling proud of himself. They both took a break to eat and then went back to cutting. The smaller man continued to disappear regularly and the strong man became annoyed. He continued cutting – almost angrily, putting all his effort into every swing of the axe, determined that his diligence would pay off.

As evening drew near, the foreman came by to survey each man's work and assign payment. The strong man, exhausted, put down his axe and stretched his tired back, waiting to be rewarded for his hard work. To his surprise, the smaller man had cleared nearly 1/3 more trees than he had! It seemed impossible. The little guy had taken breaks all day long! When the foreman left, the strong man angrily confronted the smaller man and asked him where he had been going all day. The small man wiped his brow, smiled and said, "Every forty-five minutes, I stopped to sharpen my axe." He picked up the strong man's axe and pointing to the blade he said, "When your axe gets dull, you have to work twice as hard and can only get half as much done."

How sharp is your axe?

How sharp is your sword?

I want you to get focused because there is a great reward in doing so. Hebrews 11:6 (KJV) says, "But without faith it is impossible to please Him: for he that that cometh to God must believe that He is, and that He is a rewarder of them that diligently seek Him." Many people are unable to focus on anything for more than a few days. They start a diet and give up before a week is out. They begin an exercise plan and quit when their muscles get sore. They buy books they don't read, make plans they don't keep, start projects they don't finish. Sound familiar?

If I were to ask you what your pastor or minister preached about this past Sunday at church, you probably couldn't tell me what the message was about. Or, maybe you could tell me one or two points, but couldn't give much detail about the message or how to apply it to your own life. Why? Because you probably were not focused on the message, even while you were listening. You were most likely distracted by that crying baby, or that woman's ridiculous hat or the kid who kept leaving to go to the restroom. Maybe you were thinking about what you were going to eat for lunch or were wondering about how much longer this guy was going to preach! Once you left the meeting, that was probably the last thought you gave to the message. No effort was made to meditate on the Scriptures given or to ask the Holy Spirit to give the message life inside of you. Understand, this is not a criticism – this is uncovering a symptom. A symptom of a life without focus.

Ways To Keep A Sharp Sword

What are some ways to keep a sharp sword? Please read Ephesians 6:10-18 and you will see why it is critical for you to have a sharp sword. You must realize that you are in a battle against the enemy (Satan) every day. He will try to steal, kill and destroy you. Here are just a few ways to keep your sword sharp on a daily basis.

- **Praise and Worship God:** Play a worship CD when you get up or as you drive to work and spend time in fellowship with God. Shut off the radio. Quit listening to the same old bad reports from the news, and begin to have fellowship by praising, worshiping and thanking God daily.

- **Read the Word and Confess:** Every day, spend time reading a few chapters in the Bible and speak daily confessions that will meet a specific need you are encountering. Then, take these Scriptures and write them down and confess them three to four times a day. You need to speak them out loud. The devil can't read your mind, but he can respond to your words. Charles Capps, a great minister of God, says "we are getting exactly what we are saying." If you are saying words of doubt or unbelief, then that is what you are getting — a lifestyle of defeat! Proverbs 16:24 says that pleasant words are like a honeycomb. They are sweet to the soul, and bring health to the bones. Proverbs 18:21 says "death and life are in the power of the tongue; and they that love it shall eat the fruit thereof." What fruit are you eating of? Life or death? That's why in a negative world, you need to be speaking the Word of God, the life of God over your situations. I suggest that you personalize the following

Confessions

Scriptures by putting your name into them and confessing these on a daily basis. They are; Ephesians 1:16-23, Ephesians 3:14-21, and Colossians 1:9-14.

↝ Prayer: Spend time in prayer on a daily basis. First thank God for His faithfulness and His love for you, then speak, confess and honor His name above all things. Finally, ask your requests. I pray the following prayer over my life on a daily basis:

"I am the righteousness of God in Christ Jesus (2 Corinthians 5:21), filled with the Holy Ghost and power (Acts 1:8), unto signs, wonders and miracles (Mark 16:17,20, Isaiah 8:18) through the Spirit of wisdom and revelation (Ephesians 1:17). For I have been destined and appointed to live my life for the praise of His glory! (Ephesians 1:14)."

What I would like to do, is put something in your hands that you can keep near you, keep near your Bible as a workbook that can help you stay focused over a period of time. Along with *The Focus Fulfilled Life,* I have developed a workbook. This workbook follows a process and incorporates specific Scriptures for each of the five areas; spiritual, emotional, relational, physical and financial. You decide which area to focus on. The workbook is designed to help you stick to the process described for you in this book. The workbook will help you set goals and assign tasks. It will give you key Scriptures to meditate on, memorize and activate in your life. The workbook outlines faith confessions for you to declare over specific situations. It will help you measure results and evaluate your progress. The workbook is designed to help you focus on a specific area for a period of 40 days to help you gain results.

Age Doesn't Matter

I want everyone reading this book to understand that age doesn't matter. I have seen my children focus on the things of God at a young age because my wife and I put processes in place for them to follow in order to be successful.

I will first challenge you personally, that focusing at any age is possible through the power of the Holy Spirit who is your Helper. Secondly, as a parent of children or teenagers, you have influence over them and this is a critical age to help them get focused to achieve specific goals. My wife and I sat down with our children and discussed what their goals were at a young age.

For example, I taught my children the laws of prosperity when they were young. They understood that if you want to prosper, you have got to sow to reap. My son, Daniel, had an RT 100 Yamaha dirt bike and was growing out of it. He came to me and told me he wanted a new bike and was going to invest in fixing up the RT 100 and sow it to the pastor's son as a seed for his new bike. After he did that, God provided me with a bonus and told me to invest into a newer used bike for my son and give it to him on Christmas of that year. The look on my son's face when he opened up the door and saw a new Suzuki RM 125 motorcycle was filled with joy and excitement. He later told me that he knew that if he would sow his old bike after first fixing it up and putting it in the best running condition, he would reap — and he did. My daughter has also experienced similar results. She and her husband are both living debt free, prospering and giving into the Kingdom of God at a young age because I taught them how to focus on being a blessing to others and fulfilling the covenant of Genesis 12:3 (that we have been empowered to prosper in order to be a blessing to others).

My daughter, Theresa, loved to worship, sing and dance. So what we did was get her focused on using her gifts and talents for the Lord at a young age. We enrolled her in dance classes, provided her with singing lessons, and then classes to learn how to play the keyboard. At a young age, she was leading worship in the church and on mission trips, singing and playing the keyboard and dancing before the Lord.

In Exodus 31:1-6 we read about a young man named Bezaleel who was given the awesome responsibility to build the tabernacle where the very presence of God would be made evident. Biblical theologians state that he was only thirteen years old! Can you imagine your thirteen year old son or daughter being given this responsibility? Today, you are just trying to get them to clean up their room and take the trash out!

However, God is no respecter of persons and He can use your children at a young age. I believe Bezaleel had parents that helped him focus on his destiny when he was still very young. The Bible says he was filled with the Spirit of God and was given wisdom, understanding, and knowledge in all manner of workmanship. My wife and I took our children to a church that preached present day truth, and our children were filled with the power of the Holy Spirit at a young age. There was no rebellion in our children. We never spoke that out and never accepted that lie from the enemy. Our job was to get them focused on their calling; our daughter as a worship leader/evangelist and our son with a pastoral/marketplace gifting.

When our children were 10-15 years old, they traveled across the eastern and southern areas of the United States, ministered to other kids in churches about how to worship, pray, intercede, and use flags and banners. They saw great moves of God under a program called S.W.A.T. (Spiritual Warfare Advanced Training) led by Pastors Russ and Helen Beason.

What about some of you older people who feel you do not have the energy to focus any longer to see the results God has promised you in His Word? My encouragement to you is to consider Caleb. In Joshua 14:6-13, we learn that Caleb wanted his inheritance from God at eighty-five years old. My mother is eighty-five years old this year and still works full time, still serves God visiting nursing homes, helping the poor and is as active as Caleb was. Caleb said in verse 11 that he was as strong that day as he was when he was with Moses forty years prior. Why? Because he had the power of the Spirit of God working in him and he was focused on his inheritance. He was focused on his mountain and guess what, he got it! There is an inheritance that is ours as people of God. This inheritance is abundant life on the earth, walking in victory, and being a blessing to those who need a Savior and Lord, Jesus Christ.

Why Focus 40 Days?

The number 40 is very significant in the Bible. There are several times in the Bible where a specific season of 40 days was set apart to accomplish the purpose of God in the earth.

- Genesis 7 – God caused it to rain for 40 days and 40 nights to cleanse the earth.

- Exodus 24 – Moses spent 40 days on the mountain with God and received the Ten Commandments.

- Numbers 13 – Joshua, Caleb and ten other men spent 40 days scouting the Promised Land. After 40 days, God gave Joshua the strategy to take the land.

- Deuteronomy 9 – Moses spent 40 days in repentance before the Lord because of the sins of Israel. God heard him and spared Israel.

- 1 Samuel 17 – Goliath (the enemy) taunted Israel for 40 days. After 40 days, David arrived with the wisdom and favor of God and defeated him soundly.

- 1 Kings 19 – Elisha spent 40 days with the Lord at Mount Horeb and was prepared to anoint the King of Syria, the King of Israel, and Elisha as a prophet in his place. He impacted the future of an entire nation.

- Ezekiel 4 – Ezekiel was commanded by God to lie on his right side for 40 days as a prophetic act. (This was due to the iniquity of Judah).

- Jonah 4 – Jonah prophesied, giving Ninevah 40 days to repent before the Lord. The people of Ninevah listened, repented and were spared.

- Matthew 4 (Mark 1, Luke 4) – Jesus spent 40 days in the wilderness and successfully faced temptation and the attack of Satan. This 40 days was part of his preparation for the cross.

- Acts 1 – After enduring the cross and His victorious resurrection, Jesus spent 40 days appearing to the children of Israel, providing undisputable proof of His resurrection and instructing them about the Kingdom of God. He prepared them to receive the gift of the Holy Spirit. At the end of 40 days, He ascended into heaven. The Comforter, the Holy Spirit, came in Acts 2!

We know that 40 days is very significant in the Bible. In each case, there was a specific purpose associated with a season of 40 days. We know that it takes at least 21 – 28 days to break or to create a habit. 40 days will put you over the timeline for success! When you focus on a goal for 40 days, you will experience a breakthrough.

I want to caution you. The key to success in the next 40 days is not the manifestation itself, but the ability to begin and incorporate a process in your life that eventually becomes a lifestyle of focusing on specific objectives to gain results. Don't be discouraged if a life-long problem isn't resolved at the end of 40 days. Focus on the results AND even more importantly focus on the process. At the end of 40 days you will be stronger, sharper and better equipped to face life.

How many times in your life have you put an objective out there and not been able to achieve that objective? In *The Focus Fulfilled Life*, I am creating a process for you that can help you walk through your daily life with focus, with determination and with purpose so that you will begin to see the results that you've been looking for.

What should I expect to happen?

As you focus during the next 40 days, I believe that God will speak to you and give you wisdom and insight on how to achieve manifestation. You may experience a manifestation and see specific results or breakthrough quickly. You may find that the process allows you to gain insight, wisdom and understanding that will get those results a little further down the road. The key of what to expect is to really stay focused for those 40 days. If you miss a day or two, it's okay. Don't give up or feel you must start all over again. Just get back on the program.

The only way you will be successful in your pursuit is to be in a place of expectation and faith. You must look intently and focus on specific Scriptures. You must apply those Scriptures by faith into the situations you are believing God for in order to receive a breakthrough. As you focus, the Spirit of God will rest on you. He will begin to give you insight and reveal solutions to your problems as He supernaturally opens doors of opportunity and blessing.

good for 40 day focus

What do I need to do?

Keep your eyes on God. Stay in faith and remain in a place of expectation. Know that if you do your part, God will do His part to bring about the results that you desire. You must believe God is going to move. The Bible says in 1 John 5:13-14 *AMP*, "This is the confidence (the assurance, the privilege of boldness) which we have in Him; (we are sure) that if we ask anything (make any request) according to His will (in agreement with His own plan – *the will of God is the Word of God, His last will and testament),* He listens to and hears us. And if (since) we (positively) know that He listens to us in whatever we ask, we also know (with settled and absolute knowledge) that we have (granted us as our present possessions) the requests made of Him." If you are unaccustomed to following through with a discipline, link up with someone who will hold you accountable and be willing to push you a little so that your determination defeats your distractions.

When I began to focus specifically on hearing the voice of God, things began to change in my life. I realize that you may have a very pressing concern in your life right now. You may be wrestling with a difficult or deteriorating relationship. You may be having financial pressures or be struggling with your career. You might be facing a serious health crisis and need the hand of God to miraculously heal you. No matter what the crisis, I am asking you to spend your first 40 days focusing on your relationship with God. Focus on the great and powerful Holy Spirit, who can speak to you and give you answers to all of your life situations. Begin by seeking God for wisdom and revelation. Many times we go out and do things without the wisdom of God, only to find that our best intentions and greatest efforts are without significant fruit.

> "Through skillful and godly Wisdom is a house (a life, a home, a family) built, and by understanding it is established [on a sound and good foundation],
>
> And by knowledge shall its chambers [of every area] be filled with all precious and pleasant riches."
>
> Proverbs 24:3-4 AMP

Can you imagine what would happen if you had God's insight and wisdom, through the Holy Spirit, on a daily basis? What if you were able to apply that wisdom into the situations you were concerned about and desired a breakthrough? Would you not get tremendous results? Of course you would!

As we begin this 40 days of focus, I encourage you to spend time in a quiet place every day in order to understand and to hear the voice of God. It is one thing to read the Word of God. But it is critical to obey the voice of God. When we hear God's voice, we are empowered and compelled to go out and do the things we need to do in order to fulfill our purpose. When we hear God's voice and gain His perspective, we are equipped with the things we need in order to go forth and bring forth!

"Now it shall come to pass, if you diligently obey the voice of the LORD your God, to observe carefully all His commandments which I command you today, that the LORD your God will set you high above all nations of the earth. And all these blessings shall come upon you and overtake you, because you obey the voice of the LORD your God."   Deuteronomy 28:1-2 NKJV

"The LORD your God will make you abound in all the work of your hand, in the fruit of your body, in the increase of your livestock, and in the produce of your land for good. For the LORD will again rejoice over you for good as He rejoiced over your fathers, if you obey the voice of the LORD your God, to keep His commandments and His statutes which are written in this Book of the Law, and if you turn to the LORD your God with all your heart and with all your soul."   Deuteronomy 30:9-10 NKJV

"...that you may love the LORD your God, that you may obey His voice, and that you may cling to Him, for He is your life and the length of your days; and that you may dwell in the land which the LORD swore to your fathers, to Abraham, Isaac, and Jacob, to give them."   Deuteronomy 30:20 NKJV

Setting goals is powerful. Setting goals given to you by God is even more powerful. Accomplishing tasks that are led by the Holy Spirit (and not by our flesh) produce the greatest results. When you are able to cooperate with God's purpose and desires for your life, great success is before you! I will help you establish a process, set goals, create a strategy that assigns tasks and measures results. You will need to embrace the process, energize your faith and walk confidently into your victory.

Are you ready? Let's get started!

FOCUS Points

A SUMMARY OF WHAT YOU HAVE LEARNED

Chapter Two Focus Points

- You must keep you sword sharp by spending time daily reading and confessing the Word of God, praying and spending quality time in His presence.

- God is not a respecter of persons; all who respond to Him receive His grace. God will draw nigh to anyone who calls upon His name. There are no age limitations for beginning a process for success.

- It takes 21-28 days to break or begin a habit. Forty Days of Focus will put you past this. By focusing, releasing your faith, being confident and in an attitude of expectation during the next 40 days, your objectives, goals and desires will become a reality.

Chapter Three

The PROCESS To FOCUS

The Bible says in Ephesians 6:10-18, that when we go through battles in our lives, we need to *stand* through those battles. In verse 13 it says to, "stand your ground on the evil day of danger, and having done all that the crisis demands, to stand firmly in your place." To stand means that you do not waver from your beliefs or your moral position. To stand means that you do not cave in to pressures that arise. To stand means that you are focused on the outcome and unwilling to be distracted by momentary setbacks, difficult situations or even difficult personalities you encounter. Standing is not only important during times of crisis, but standing is VITAL to your success when it comes to believing for a manifestation of God's blessing in a particular area of your life. You must be able to articulate what you are believing God for. Then you must be able to confess the promises of God over that situation and stand on those promises. You must begin to apply the Word of God in that situation as you focus on the result you desire. You must STAND on the ground of success. You must picture the thing as accomplished and STAND in a place of victory until reality aligns itself with the position you have chosen to stand on!

I sought the Lord concerning the struggle I saw others going through and how many of them never seemed to experience victory. The Lord revealed to me that most people do not stand long enough to get the victory. Victory is within their grasp, but like a long distance runner who quits just before breaking the tape, they give up too soon and suffer bitter disappointment. I've had personal situations in my own life, where I have had

> **People do not STAND long enough to get the VICTORY**

to stand for a short period of time to receive victory. An example of this is the testimony I gave earlier about my brother, Jim Sanderbeck. I stood and walked the floor, crying out to God for him and focused on his healing. Within one week, God had answered our prayers and given Jim a complete, total and miraculous victory.

In 1981, my daughter was born with a Strep B infection in my wife's uterine canal. They took her to a children's hospital, and cautioned us that 80% of children having this virus die. Well, I had to stand on God's Word. I pulled out my Bible and began to confess Isaiah 53:4-5 and Psalm 107:20. I began to stand on God's Word for the wholeness of my daughter. Within ten days, she was released from the hospital, the virus was destroyed and my daughter grew up completely whole.

In 1993, my wife was diagnosed with potential uterine cancer. They looked at the cells and told her that she should have cancer. We had to believe God for the total wholeness of her body. She came through a minor operation and has had no more problems since. But that took a release of my faith and a focus on her wholeness in order to see victory.

But many other times, I have been required to stand for a long period of time. In 1995, I was downsized from my position with a major Fortune 500 company. For the next three years, I was put to the test to see if I really trusted the Provider. I brought forth an idea that the Lord gave me to an already established company. Based on my idea, we worked together to create new materials and change their existing materials to meet the needs of college students. I went from a healthy, six-figure income to almost no income at all for the first year. Prior to being downsized, I spent a long period of time focusing on and standing on God as my Provider. I was prepared in my heart and in my spirit. Every day during this time I was able to see the hand of God at work. So, although this was a testing of my faith, when the evil day came, I was able to stand and believe God. I had to walk out my faith believing that the idea I received was from God. I had big financial expectations on this idea, but didn't experience financial fruit until after the first one and a half years in this business. It was a slow process of teaching me to trust the Provider since the financial results did not meet my expectations in the first 18 months. Was God blessing it? Yes, but I had to endure the process to get it up and running before I could see the greater success. We had to get this program into a test market format before it became a reality in the college freshman orientation realm and helped colleges retain students.

I experienced frustration because I knew this idea was from God, but felt I was not being compensated fairly. After three years of sacrificing time, energy and living off a small financial base provided by the employer, my wife and I began to focus on what God was saying. Either I was going to be blessed here with this idea, or God was going to move me out. I sowed a $1,000 seed to a ministry, and named my seed, expecting the harvest from this seed to move me toward my destiny. Within a month, I received a call from the Fortune 500 Company I was downsized from

he had to wait 1½ yr.

39

and was offered a position. Not only that, but they asked me to come back, restoring my tenure, full benefits, and a six figure income.

I now had a dilemma. Should I stay where I was putting my God-given idea into practice, but was not getting compensated fairly, or move on to where God had repositioned me back to the Fortune 500 Company? I decided to return to the Fortune 500 company, leaving my idea behind without receiving the promised compensation. This was a tough decision, I had suffered a wrong and could very easily justify anger or allowed bitterness. Instead of getting offended, I decided to tell the Lord about it. I sowed this idea to them and I named my seed. My expectation for this seed was to reap a greater harvest from the idea I sowed to them. Since that time, God has been faithful in bringing me harvest after harvest, based on my attitude and my focused mentality on sowing a seed and not becoming offended. My heart was to bless that company and the man behind it. Sowing a seed of that magnitude will only produce for me when I sow in love, seed sown in anger or strife is rendered useless.

In fact, for at least one situation, I have been standing on God's healing promises for more than **7 1/2** years when my son was in an accident — and I am STILL standing, unwavering in my faith that what God has spoken over this situation WILL come to pass! While I stand, I have experienced several breakthroughs in this area, and I am encouraged every time that God brings us one step closer to complete victory.

If you are discouraged, consider Job. What Job feared came upon him and his family. He had a fear that his sons and daughters would curse God and that something terrible would happen to them. However, God in His mercy to Job was able to hear his cry and redeem him. Here was a man who had everything taken from him, even though he was a righteous servant of God. His friends came around him and instead of offering encouragement and support, they offered all manner of foolishness — even rebuke. Job's answers to them were filled with faith and trust in God. Even in the face of total misery, he trusted God. Even when everyone around him, including his wife, urged him to curse God, Job did not. He stood. The Bible records that God restored everything to him in a double portion and that the latter part of his life was much greater than the early part. Job stood — and God gave him victory!

When you stand, be prepared for the response of others around you who may not understand your position or your faith. I strongly encourage you to find someone who supports you (covenant people) to help keep you accountable and to stand *with* you. Limit your fellowship with those who empower the wrong things in your life or who speak negatively. Apostle John Kelly says, "Go where you're celebrated — not just tolerated." Spend time with people who share your faith and support your vision. When you begin to focus, you will quickly discover who is truly in covenant with you and who is just "hanging around." If focusing was easy, if standing was easy — then many more people would experience regular success. I am not promising a quick fix or an easy solution. Focus is a process that requires discipline and determination. What I can promise is that if you will do the difficult, God will do the impossible!

I have created an acronym for the words FOCUS and STAND. I want to walk you through what each letter stands for. The purpose of this is to help you remember some key elements in days to come as you embrace the process and begin your journey to a Focus Fulfilled Life.

FOCUS

F — FAITH: *I have been given a measure of faith (Romans 12:3). I must release my faith to God so that He can hear my prayer. Even if my faith is as small as a tiny mustard seed - it is enough faith to move mountains and NOTHING is IMPOSSIBLE (Matthew 17:20). Faith is critical in the process of being focused.*

> "NOW FAITH is the assurance, the confirmation, the title deed, of the things we hope for, being the proof of things we do not see and the conviction of their reality, faith perceiving as real fact what is not revealed to the senses."
>
> Hebrews 11:1 AMP

You are not able to see faith. Faith is not part of your physical senses. The Bible says, "Now, faith is..." So, faith is always constant. If you are going to walk in the process of staying focused, you must identify what faith is.

FAITH: being fully persuaded that God is going to meet my need.

My definition for the word faith is this: that I am fully persuaded that God is going to meet my need. In this same chapter of Hebrews, the Bible also says that faith is the substance. It doesn't say that faith is A substance, but rather that faith is THE substance. Faith is THE substance of things hoped for. The substance I am speaking of is the foundation of God's Word. The will of God begins with the Word of God. God's will is for you to prosper and to be successful. The Bible says in Jeremiah 29:11 *AMP*, "For I know the thoughts and plans that I have for you, says the Lord, thoughts and plans for welfare and peace and not for evil, to give you hope in your final outcome."

You need to understand that if you are fully persuaded, and have confidence in this substance, the foundation of God's Word, then you must have a hope. A *'Bible Hope'* is an earnest expectation with an outstretched neck. In your mind, picture a horse. This horse sees you coming toward him with a sugar cube and sticks his head through the fence and stretches his neck as far toward you as possible — anticipating and expecting that you are going to give him a taste of that delicious sugar cube! Just like the horse that sees you coming and knows that the sugar cube is his — you also need to have this same eager anticipation, this same hope with expectation. When you have faith with expectation, you lean into the promise; just like the horse stretching his neck through the fence. You know it's coming and you are eager with anticipation to receive the promise! If you are going to be able to get what you need to have in a Focus Fulfilled Life, you must have faith.

O — OPPORTUNITY: *I have the opportunity to share Jesus daily. Every day that I go out into the world and into my sphere of influence and authority, I will find opportunities.*

The majority of us are not full-time paid staff members of a church or ministry. Most of us work in the secular world. In my own life, I view every situation that arises and every encounter with another human being, as an opportunity for me to prove that God's Word works for me! For the past thirty years, I have worked in Fortune 500 Companies, and have viewed my business as my ministry. We deal with a hurting world and people without God do not have hope — the 'Bible Hope' of an earnest expectation. When my son was in an accident, he was without oxygen for twelve minutes and in a coma for eight weeks. Even during our own time of stress, my wife and I were able to minister to people in the intensive care unit who didn't have a relationship with the Lord. They were looking for someone to minister to them. Guess what we did? That's right. We began to minister to these individuals because we knew it was just another opportunity to prove the Word of God. (If you want to see fruit in your life as a witness for the Lord, go hang outside of a hospital and just ask people if they need prayer). Because I am so focused on being seed-minded and not need-minded, my wife and I sowed seeds of love and compassion toward these people, knowing we would reap the harvest for our son!

One situation we encountered was a family moving to another state, and the mother had a massive stroke. She was on her deathbed. We asked her husband if we could pray for her before they pulled the plug. All her family flew in and came to the hospital. They gathered around her as my wife went to the top of her head and ministered the love of Jesus and asked her to rededicate herself to the Lord, whispering in her ear. I know we are a spirit, that we have a soul (emotions, will, and intellect), and that we live in a body that eventually grows old. But her spirit was catching what Cindy was praying and a peace came over her. The family was weeping, but an unmistakable spirit of joy entered the room as they grasped the reality that she was soon going to be in heaven, wrapped in the arms of Jesus. This was an opportunity for us to be a blessing to this family and be part of her homecoming into heaven. So, no matter what you are going through in life, you must become sensitive to hear God's voice in these opportunities.

C - CHRIST CENTERED: *I must put Christ first today and I must hear His voice. Being Christ centered is central to my success.*

In Ephesians 4:23-27, the Bible says that we are to strip off our old man and put on a new, fresh mental attitude.

It says to give no place to the devil, but to remain Christ centered and literally to 'put on' Christ daily. Every day you must strip off your old man and put on the new man.

Many people are paralyzed by their past. My dear friend, Patrick Ondrey, gave a message entitled, "Don't Park Here." The basic premise was that we are hindered not only by our past failure, but even by our past success. Yesterday is a distraction! Each new day needs to be encountered with a fresh perspective and new goals, met with a fresh anticipation and embraced with zest. Each day, place Christ at the center of all you do. This doesn't mean you speak in "Christian-ese" or spew Scripture at every person you meet. What it does mean is that you have the mind of Christ at work within you. It means that His nature and His character are reflected through you. When Christ is your center, you are a wellspring of life, joy and peace. Your problems are put into perspective and you can live in the security of knowing that your final outcome is highly favorable.

The Bible clearly teaches us how to stop Satan and to become more Christ Centered.

"Leave no (such) room or foothold for the devil (give no opportunity to him)."
                              Ephesians 4.27 AMP

"Submit yourself therefore to God. Resist the devil, and he will flee from you."
                              James 4.7 KJV

"We know that whosoever is born of God sinneth not; but he that is begotten of God keepeth himself, and that the wicked one toucheth him not."
                              1 John 5.18 KJV

The FOCUS FULFILLED *Life*

the word of God is living and active

U- USE IT AND DO IT: *I must use the principles of God on a daily basis and apply these principles to my life.*

You can't apply what you don't know! That is why it is so important for you to get in God's Word on a daily basis. To have success in a particular area of your life, you need to gather Scriptures that pertain to this area, and apply those Scriptures to the situations you are believing God for. If you have a physical need in your body, then identify Scriptures that speak about healing so you can stand on the promise for wholeness. Sow those Scriptures into your physical body by confessing them out loud — and you will see a change!

In the workbook that goes with *The Focus Fulfilled Life*, I have outlined many Scriptures that deal with specific areas such as physical, emotional, relational and financial areas. As you go through a particular workbook that sets definite goals, part of the process is to meditate on and confess specific Scriptures that speak to your area of need. As you do this, the Word of God quickens life (Hebrews 4:12) inside of you and brings wisdom and understanding for how to deal successfully in the area you are focusing on. Use it and do it. It is why God gave us His Word!

S- STRATEGIES FOR SUCCESS: *I will apply the strategies that God gives me today in order to see success.*

God is a strategic God and He desires to give you strategies on a daily basis to gain success. When you look back at the Old and New Testament, there were always strategies for success. When Joshua came in and pulled down the walls of Jericho, there was a strategy given to him by God to accomplish this. God told them to walk around the city for seven days and then to shout on that seventh day and the walls came down.

When we don't know......

In my job, I needed a strategy to sell more orange juice. I realized that what worked last year was not going to work this year. Due to hurricanes and pests destroying the crop, the orange crop was at its lowest yield in twenty years. What I needed to do, was to ask the Lord to show me how I was going to meet my objectives with the plan that the company presented to me. In the natural, this was impossible. However, by hearing the voice of God behind His Word, I tapped into His strategies for success. According to James 1:5, if we lack wisdom, we can ask for it and the Lord will give it to us. In Proverbs 16:3 and 16:9, we see that if we commit our works to the Lord (spiritual and natural), our thoughts will be established, and He will direct our paths. In the past three years, I have cried out for more wisdom and strategies that would produce the greatest results for the company I work for, as well as strategies to bless me and my counterparts in the process.

The majority of my bonus is based on what we all do as a team, so my prayer was for God to release strategies over the entire team so we could all prosper. My heart is to build the Kingdom of God through my finances. Because of this I receive more so I can sow more! In the past three years, I have made over six figures just in bonuses because I am praying and focusing on strategies to bless my team so I can prosper to bless and build the Kingdom of God. In order to do this, God has to prosper me! Why, because I am a giver according to 2 Corinthians 9:10. God supplies seed to the sower, not to those who will hoard it up for their own desires. My wife and I are sowers and with the strategies that come from the Lord, there will be a harvest for us to be a blessing on every occasion. Again, my strategy for success is being seed-minded, not need-minded. I am not looking for someone to meet my need. When I go to the office or to church, I am conscious and aware that I have been empowered to prosper in all things so I can be a blessing to others by fulfilling the covenant of Genesis 12:2-3. You need to apply

2 Corinthians 9:5 - 15

the strategies that God gives you each day and you will also be able to see greater success.

STAND

"Therefore put on the full armor of God, so that when the day of evil comes, you may be able to stand your ground, and after you have done everything, to stand." Ephesians 6:13 NIV

We need to stand every day and believe God. I have also created an acronym for the word stand to help you endure, prevail, continue and remain in a place of focus until you receive the victory and achieve success!

S - STAY IN THE SPIRIT: *I must be controlled by the Spirit of God. It is critical that I remain responsive to the Holy Spirit and be directed and guided by Him. "So I say, live by the Spirit, and you will not gratify the desires of the sinful nature. Galatians 5:16* NIV

Are you easily distracted? Do you find it difficult to pray for more than a few minutes? Do you mean to spend time meditating on God and His Word, but find your mind wandering or fall asleep? You are not alone! Many people find it very difficult to stay in the Spirit. I want to help you create a lifestyle of focus that makes you more responsive to the Holy Spirit. This is the primary reason why I encourage you to take the first 40 days to focus on your relationship with the Holy Spirit. Then, as you begin to take focus on your objectives, goals and strategies for specific areas in your life, you are going to be able to hear the voice of God more clearly and become more responsive to His Spirit.

I believe that if we can stay in the Spirit and stay above all the distractions of this world, we will always gain the victory. When you are controlled by the Spirit, this means that the Holy Spirit has power over you and that He influences every decision. Just recently the Lord told me that when I enter into the weaknesses of my flesh, I am empowering the enemy instead of calling upon the Spirit to control and guide me. Jesus already dealt with Satan and deprived him of his power over us, so when I enter into sin, I empower the enemy instead of empowering the Holy Spirit to help me overcome my weakness. When I am weak, then in Him I am strong. "Let the weak (say) I am strong!" Joel 3:10. When you are directed by the Spirit, this means that the Holy Spirit regulates your activities and the course of your life. When you are guided by the Holy Spirit, this means that you allow Him to show you the best way to go. **Stay in the Spirit!**

Bible instructs us on how to speak

T - THANKSGIVING: *I will continually thank God for all His blessings. I will operate in a mindset of gratitude.*

Deuteronomy 28 is a chapter of blessing and also a chapter of curse. The Bible says in Deut 28:47-48 *AMP*, "Because you did not serve the Lord your God with joyfulness of mind and heart in gratitude for the abundance of all with which He had blessed you, therefore you shall serve your enemies whom the Lord shall send against you, in hunger and thirst, in nakedness and in want of all things." Thankfulness is an important key to being able to stand. Without gratitude in your spirit, an attitude of negativity will creep in and destroy your focus.

Have you ever noticed that some people seem to have a dark cloud over their heads all the time? No matter what, these people seem to experience the worse case scenario for every life situation. The truth is that when you are negative and ungrateful, you tend to draw bad things around you. You see the bad and expect the worst. You speak, "just my luck," and the bad scenario in your mind comes to pass. There is no such thing as luck, since all things come from God. The Lord wants us to have a thankful heart. He wants us to walk in gratitude and look for the good in things. In fact, He told us, "In everything give thanks; for this is the will of God in Christ Jesus for you." 1 Thessalonians 5:18 *NKJV*

So, in this process of focus and creating a lifestyle of being focused, I want you to stay in the Spirit and be in a place of thanksgiving every day. Thank God for all He has done for you and for all His blessings. Thank others in your life and become truly grateful for every good thing around you. As you do this, you will find that your countenance becomes brighter. You will begin to notice blessings that you were once taking for granted. The Bible tells us in Genesis 12:2-3 that we have been empowered to prosper in order to be a blessing to others. So, let's thank God for the blessings He has given us, and become a blessing to others around us. The transformation in your life will be amazing!

A - APPLY THE PRINCIPLES: *I will apply the principles that I have learned. When I study God's Word, this brings God's revelation knowledge to me. This helps me be able to apply the principles of God to every area of my life.*

Take for instance, the principle of seedtime and harvest found in Mark 4. If you sow strife to somebody, you're going to reap strife. If you sow love, you're going to reap love. When I encounter a situation of disagreement, I look at the negative action and sow the opposite, positive action. If they are sowing strife and things that are negative, I'm going to come in and sow love. If I respond with strife, I'm going to reap that somewhere else in my life later on. I am not bound by inappropriate, disrespectful, or harmful actions by another individual. I CAN sow the opposite seed, determining a positive future for myself even in the midst of a negative or difficult situation. I have never done this without seeing things begin to change. It seems there is more strife in family relationships today than ever before. So, when you find yourself in the midst of a situation filled with strife, then to bring change to the situation, you must sow love. That is how you counter any negative thought or area of strife and division. Sow the opposite spirit and you will see tremendous results come forth.

apply this to any area ←

There are many principles in God's Word that are relevant to your life. You must know what the principles of God are and apply them. Mark 4 is also important when you focus on the financial aspect of your life. The Bible says in Romans 13:8, "owe no man anything but to love him." In other words, stay out of debt! I realize that there are times when you have the financial provision to purchase something on credit and pay it off over a short period of time, but to have credit card debt of $5,000 - $20,000 is not God's plan. I have no mortgage on my house, and I am using that property as an investment to gain wealth. This strategy is a positive way to pay back a minimal second mortgage (or home equity line of credit) of 5-7% while you are making 10-20% on investments. I am becoming a wealth builder so I can become a wealth distributor and build the Kingdom of God. I am focused on applying Biblical principles to build wealth, so I can be a blessing to others and see the Kingdom of God advanced. All you need to do is focus on gaining an understanding of how the Kingdom of God operates and be a doer of it to see success.

Quote this

N - NO PLACE TO THE DEVIL: *I will give no place to the devil today (Ephesians 4:27). I declare that his strategies are negated.*

Ephesians 4:27 tells us to give no place to the devil, and in the verse before this, it admonishes us to not let the sun go down on our wrath. Anger and bitterness sabotage more believers than drugs, sex or alcohol combined! When believers allow anger to simmer inside them unresolved and give root to bitterness, they give the devil an opportunity to enter their lives. Don't let the sun go down on your anger. This means that you keep short accounts. You don't stew over wrongs committed against you. You are not easily offended and you waste no time rehearsing what you *wish* you *would* have said. Give no place to the devil!

My pastor, Michael Bruno, encourages us to begin the day by saying, "The strategies of hell are negated over the people in our church, and the strategies of God are loosed upon the people of our church." When you begin to declare things like this, it brings life to you and helps you remain focused as you pray for other people. It is amazing how many of your own problems will be resolved when you become the solution to someone else's problem.

D- DELIGHT MYSELF IN GOD: *I will delight myself in the Lord today and He will give me the desires of my heart (Psalm 37:4).*

How do you delight yourself in the Lord? It begins with acknowledging Him as your Creator, your Savior and your Lord. Consider Him. Think about His goodness, His lovingkindness, His mercy toward you, His faithfulness.... Praise Him! Bow yourself to Him in worship. Tell Him what you think of Him. Speak out loud that you love Him and that you are awed by His presence. Enjoy His presence! I know of no greater way to delight in God than to spend time alone with Him or in the congregation of His people, honoring Him with your praise and worship.

The more you delight in Him, the more your desires align with His. As your heart yields to Him and your desires align with His will, He easily gives you the desires of your heart because they accomplish His purpose in your life.

Keys Needed to Create a Lifestyle of Focus

- ☞ I recommend that you focus for 40 days. I mentioned before that it takes 21 – 28 days to break or to establish a habit. 40 days gets you well beyond this. I also outlined several examples of powerful 40 day periods in the Bible. I have exercised this practice of focusing for a period of 40 days many times and experienced tremendous success. Forty days creates a fullness of the process.

- ☞ Each quarter, there is an average of 90 days. Divide the year into four quarters. What would life be like for you, if each quarter of the year you were able to focus for 40 of those 90 days on specific objectives in your life? What if you regularly and specifically focused on objectives that could even be a part of fulfilling your destiny? A Focus Fulfilled Life is within reach.

- ☞ If you were to focus on a specific area for 40 out of 90 days each quarter, in one year would you not see amazing results? This means that for 160 days out of 365 days, you would be focusing on specific things. If you will discipline yourself and focus, as you apply the Word of God, those things WILL come to pass AND produce a manifestation. Greater results. Greater success — all because you decided to focus.

FOCUS Points

A SUMMARY OF WHAT YOU HAVE LEARNED

Chapter Three Focus Points

☛ You must focus and stand for the manifestation by applying the following acronyms on a daily basis.

FOCUS

Faith

Opportunities

Christ Centered

Use It and Do It

Strategies for Success

STAND

Stay in the Spirit

Thanksgiving

Apply the Principles

No Place to the Devil

Delight Myself in God

Chapter Four

WHAT Do I Need To FOCUS On?

Most people are unable to focus for more than a few days on specific areas in their life where they need a manifestation. In fact, not only is it difficult to focus on an area that needs change, most people are not even fully aware of what their needs are. They are frustrated and disappointed with where their life is headed — their relationships, their job, their finances, their weight, their health... They don't feel successful, but have no idea how to turn things around. You may find yourself in this same position. Before you can begin to focus on a specific objective, you must understand what your basic needs are. You must take a 'Needs Assessment' — identifying areas of weakness, limitation or shortcomings that are holding you back from walking in success and victory.

Earlier in this book, we covered sowing a specific seed and naming that seed with an expectation to reap a specific harvest of blessing in your life. But, before you can sow a specific seed and truly focus on something, you must know what needs you have and what your goals are in relationship to overcoming this need.   Before going any further in this book, I am asking you to complete an important exercise. I want you to take a Needs Assessment right now and identify the areas in your life where you want to see a change. I want you to write down the things that worked for you in the past where you saw success and also write down the areas in your life where you do not have success.

As you take a Needs Assessment for your life, ask yourself some questions such as, "Where is my greatest weakness?" We all have weaknesses in our life, but if there are specific weaknesses that you have been dealing with for a long period of time, identify what those weaknesses are. You have to identify your areas of weakness before you can turn them into strengths.

Ask yourself, "What areas do I desire to grow in?" Ask, "What areas do I feel God is showing me He wants me to develop?" I am giving you a sample outline below to help guide you through the Needs Assessment. Don't get stuck trying to fill in all the blanks, but take the time to carefully consider your needs and write them down. You need to save this. We will refer back to this Needs Assessment as we proceed with the process identifying what area you need to focus on, creating objectives and setting goals to see success.

NEEDS ASSESSMENT

Where is my greatest weakness?

What area(s) do I desire to grow in?

What area(s) do I feel God is showing me to develop?

1. **Identify the Area of Need:**
   - **Spiritual:** Relationship with God, Spiritual Disciplines, Spiritual Habits, Knowledge of the Word, Practical Application of the Word in your Life, Use of Spiritual Gifts, Overcoming Fear, Overcoming Doubt, Witnessing...

   - **Emotional (Soul):** Battles in your Mind, Self-Image, Problems with Anger, Depression, Shyness or other "Soul" Issues, Lack of Education, Lack of Skills, Overcoming Generational Bondages, Yielding to Temptation...

   - **Physical (Body):** Overweight or Overeating, Health Problems, Illness or Injuries, Damaging Habits, Dealing with Stress...

   - **Social:** Difficult Relationships with your Spouse, Children, Parents or Siblings, In-Laws, Co-Workers, Employers...

   - **Financial:** Overcoming Debt, Struggles with Tithing, Fear of Giving and Not Receiving, Giving Habits, No Planning for the Future, Unclear Financial Goals, Unsuccessful or Unsatisfying Career...

2. **Identify the Specific Need:**
   - **Examples:**
     - **Spiritual:**
       I have trouble understanding the Word.
       I believe I have a gift of healing and want to see this developed.
       I have difficulty expressing praise or worship to God.
       I have no daily devotional habit...

o **Emotional (Soul):**
  I fly off the handle and yell about everything.
  I struggle with lust or pornography –
      fantasizing.
  Others make me feel inferior.
  I am depressed all the time...

o **Physical:**
  I am overweight.
  I am unsuccessful at dieting.
  I don't exercise.
  I have been diagnosed with _____
      - I need healing in my body!...

o **Social:**
  My relationship with my spouse is strained.
  I feel like my kids control my home.
  I feel unsuccessful as a parent
      and ill-equipped.
  My co-workers take advantage of me.
  My in-laws make me feel guilty if we don't
      spend every holiday with them...

o **Financial:**
  I have $_____ in credit card debt.
  I struggle tithing – I need to pay my bills.
  I want to give, but never seem to have enough
      money to give what I feel called to.
  I hate my job and it doesn't make enough
      money...

3. **Identify what you would LIKE to see in this area:**
   - **Examples:**
     - o **Spiritual:**

       I would like greater wisdom and more understanding of God's Word.

       I would like to experience more of God's Presence.

       I want to hear the voice of God...

     - o **Emotional:**

       I would like a better relationship with _____.

       I would like to control my temper.

       I want a positive self-image...

     - o **Physical:**

       I want to lose _____ lbs.

       I want healing for _____.

       —I understand that I must change _____ in order for this healing to remain successful...

     - o **Financial:**

       I want to be completely debt free!

       I want to give $ _____to the Kingdom this year.

       I want to begin investing and create a financial plan for my future.

       I want to leave an inheritance to my children and grandchildren...

There was a time in my life where I realized that I had a prophetic anointing, but knew that I needed to focus on this specific area of gifting in my life if I was going to be effective. In order to sharpen this gift, I needed to increase my understanding of the prophetic and have opportunities to develop this gift while under proper covering. I took classes at my local church on prophetic gifting. I studied how to speak prophetically into people's lives and how to hear the voice of God. I studied the Word and gained an understanding of Scripture on the subject. In the classroom setting, I began to speak prophetically over people, and with guidance I learned exactly what to do. I invested my time and energy in that specific area of gifting that God was telling me to focus on. I spent time in a classroom, I spent time one on one with individuals practicing hearing the voice of God and speaking it, and I began to utilize small care group (or home group) ministries where I was able to activate the gift. I had to focus on that gift for a period of time until I became proficient with it. I stayed submitted to my spiritual covering and allowed them to direct and correct me as the prophetic gift in me became a reality in my life and I was confident to utilize this gift.

I am asking you to complete a Needs Assessment in order to identify specific needs in your life where you have issues. I like what Gloria Copeland says, "If you have a specific need in a certain area, then you need to get Scripture, write it down and apply it to that certain area." You shouldn't be spending time focused on finances when you have a pressing need for healing in your physical body. If healing is your greatest need, then you should spend the majority of your time speaking and confessing the Word and releasing your faith with healing Scriptures. Scriptures such as Exodus 15:26 (I am the Lord who heals you), Isaiah 53:4-5, (He was wounded for my transgression...by His stripes I am healed) Psalm 107:20, (He sent His Word and healed them), 1 Peter 2:24 (He bore my sin in His own body

– by His stripes I am healed), Matthew 8:17 (He took my infirmity and bore my sickness) — You would take these and other Scriptures and begin to focus on healing. You would educate yourself on what foods you should eat and what foods you should stay away from. You would learn what types of exercise and rest habits will give you the best success. Why ask God for healing if you make no plans to keep from getting sick again? So, if healing is the greatest need in your life at this time, focus on this area. Utilize the Scripture, apply your faith, be diligent in doing what is in YOUR power for health, confess the Word of God over it and see a manifestation!

This strategy applies to every area of your life: spiritual, emotional, physical, social and financial. Each time I have experienced the greatest success in my life, it has come as a result of spending time gathering Scriptures pertinent to the area of my need, focusing the Scriptures into that situation and applying the wisdom of God in that area. The Word of God will not return void. It will accomplish the purpose and plan for what it was sent (Isaiah 55:11). But in order to be effective, the Word must be applied into a situation on a consistent, daily basis.

As you complete the Needs Assessment, the next step is to take this information and identify what specific area you need to focus on.

FIVE KEY AREAS OF FOCUS

We are a spirit, we have a soul and we live in a body. We operate in a social and a financial realm. When you begin to identify the specific needs you have, they will fall into one of five specific areas of strength or weakness for you. What are the key areas you might want to focus on?

Spiritual

If the greatest need you identified fell in this area, then you need to focus on developing your prayer life, confession, your study/devotion/meditation, your spiritual gifts or any other specific area in your spiritual life that can help you grow spiritually over the next forty days.

In chapter one, I shared with you about the time I was focusing on receiving increased wisdom and revelation from God. As I focused and applied the Word of God, I received great encouragement and confirmation from a great woman of God named Fushia Pickett. She told me that the Teacher was on duty. She told me that in order to experience growth in my spiritual life, I would have to allow the Teacher to speak to me. I would have to focus on listening to the voice of the Spirit by giving Him first place in my life and respecting Him to speak to me. To do this, I would have to quiet my soul. I needed to get into a quiet place so I could position myself to hear from God. For me, quieting my soul took a minimum of an hour. I needed an hour alone before I was free from the activities occupying my mind and could stop mentally working through what I needed to accomplish. Only when my soul was quiet and my mind clear was I able to focus on what He was saying to me. Each time I got alone to focus on hearing God's voice, it amazed me at how many tasks started pumping through my head. So, quieting my soul became a discipline with me in order to develop spiritual growth.

Just recently, I was discussing this with a close friend of mine who I have mentored over the years. He is between jobs and is frustrated because things are not going the way he expected. After more discussion with him, he finally admitted that he has been disobedient to God. He said the Lord told him to get back to the quiet place where he used to go to and listen to the voice of God. This place was a field near where he lives. Now he can't find the time to get away. He has too many tasks to accomplish before he can spend time in the field. He told me that he has to cut the grass, trim the hedges, cut wood and a list of other things that were really just excuses. The Lord spoke to me and told me to tell him that he valued the tasks he needed to do more that he valued the Presence of God! He immediately repented and said, "Looks like I'm headed up to the field this afternoon." I told him God would speak to him and tell him where to go to get that new job. Instead of sending out 200 resumes (which is not bad to do), listen to God and follow His direction. Within a week, my friend had a new job. One Word from God can change your life forever!

The point to remember is this: It took focus for me to be able to get in the Word, meditate on specific Scriptures and have the Holy Spirit teach me what the Scripture meant. After that, it took even more focus and discipline to go from understanding the Scripture to applying the Scripture to my life and becoming a doer of God's Word. Listening to God is the most important skill you will ever develop. The success of every other area in your life is dependent upon being able to hear and respond to the voice of God.

From your Needs Assessment, you should have identified specific areas in your spiritual growth that you need to focus on. These areas can take you to the next level. I encourage you to allow the Spirit of God to begin speaking to you in those specific areas.

Emotional:
(Soul — Emotions/Will/Intellect)

Your soul is comprised of your emotions, your will and your intellect. The soul is one of the most difficult areas to remain submitted to the Holy Spirit. The soul is naturally 'in the flesh' or carnal. It takes awareness and a purposeful response in order to keep the soul in submission. As you completed your Needs Assessment, you may have identified areas within your soul that have a weakness. Issues in your soul may be rooted in pride, arrogance, doubt, unbelief, fear, frustration, anger, depression, etc. These things will continue to affect your emotions, your will or your intellect as long as your soul is not directed by your spirit. People who live their lives directed by their soul are often held captive by their own emotions. I have met people who were handicapped spiritually because they were focused on their superior intellect, or so independent that they couldn't rely on anyone but themselves — not even God. People who allow their emotions, their will and intellect to take over are going to have some serious problems. It is important to focus on specific areas of your life that will bring your soul in subjection to your spirit man.

In my life, I began to see areas in my soul that were impacted by generational influences that were affecting how I lived my life. In my seed line, there were many individuals who were very manipulative and controlling. I noticed that I had the very same tendencies and was able to identify this as an area of weakness that was keeping me from reaching my full potential. So, if I was going to walk in the Spirit and not allow my soul to dictate my life, I had to utilize the Word of God, speak Scriptures and confess the Word of God over my life in those areas. I became accountable to others in covenant with me to help guard my soul. They spoke into my life whenever I began to yield to this generational stronghold. I had to focus on this area and work through a process for victory.

I have encountered many who struggle with a spirit of fear. God told us in 2 Corinthians 1:7 that He did not give us a spirit of fear, but of power, of love and a sound mind. The enemy uses fear to paralyze people from stepping out in faith. When we are afraid of failure, afraid of pain, afraid of rejection, we become filled with doubt and unbelief and unwilling to trust the promises of God. Fear and doubt keep many from experiencing victory. Faith is the only antidote to unbelief. The Bible tells us that perfect love casts out fear (I John 4:18) — and God is the ONLY source of perfect love. We cannot walk in fear and walk in victory at the same time. We must accept one and reject the other. We must become fully persuaded under the foundation and confidence of God's Word. We must have the expectation that our soul *will* come under submission to our spirit and be renewed. The Bible says in Romans 12:1-2 *NKJV*, "I beseech you therefore, brethren, by the mercies of God, that you present your bodies a living sacrifice, holy, acceptable to God, which is your reasonable service. And do not be conformed to this world, but be transformed by the renewing of your mind, that you may prove what is that good and acceptable and perfect will of God."

I want to make sure that my life proves God's Word which is good, acceptable and perfect. I want to prove God's perfect will. I understand that that the Word of God is the will of God. And so, if I can understand God's Word then I can understand God's will. If I can apply God's Word to my life, I can operate inside God's will. When I operate inside the will of God, there is no other option but success!

Renew Your Mind

The key to a focus fulfilled lifestyle is to walk in a Kingdom mindset. Jesus came preaching the Kingdom of God. In John 3:3, Jesus said, "Verily, verily, I say unto thee, except a man be born again, he cannot see the Kingdom of God." Matthew 6:33 says, "Seek first the Kingdom of God and His righteousness (His way of doing and being right)," and then all these things will be added to you. It is all about the Kingdom of God. Therefore, you must walk in a Kingdom mindset, knowing who you are in Him. We reign as a king in life because of the life, death and resurrection of Jesus (Romans 5:17 *AMP*). To have victory over an area in your soul, you must renew your mind. I once heard that we need to be *brainwashed* because our brains need to be washed by the Word of God. Ephesians 5:26 *NKJV* says, "that He might sanctify and cleanse her (the church) with the washing of water by the Word." Just as you need to take a shower and cleanse your physical body, understand that you need to wash your soul daily with the water of God's Word.   The soul is complex. You probably have many issues in your life related to past experiences, generational influences, memories, and even tied to emotional wounds or scars. As you focus on this area, you will have to allow the Holy Spirit to bring healing and release to these issues. You will have to submit to the Word of God, refuse to assume a victim mentality and focus on how to have wholeness in your soul. You want your soul — your emotions, your will and your intellect to be productive. Your soul is a gift from God. It is here where your creativity surfaces and is expressed, it is here that your intelligence thrives as you assimilate information and develop skills that help you fulfill your purpose. Is it any wonder that Satan desires to keep you crippled and bound in your soul?

Physical:
(Body)

Many times we allow our body to dominate or control us in terms of our eating habits, exercise habits, rest habits and the ability to release stress. I get a physical once a year. I do this so that I know what is required from me and what I need to focus on in terms of maintaining good health. My career produces stress. Only I can determine how I respond to this stress. It is up to me to find ways to reduce the effects of that stress through exercise, healthy eating, proper rest and focusing on God's Word in my body. In the past few years, I have been able to reduce medication for high blood pressure. I focus on working out and developing other key areas in my life which include diet, proper rest and a healthy lifestyle.

How do you take your body and bring it under submission to the Word of God? Growing older is a fact of life. Living in a fast paced, high stress, toxic environment is inevitable for most of us. On top of this, every time you turn on the TV you see that somebody has a pill for something. It is ridiculous. You can get a pill to take care of every physical need from too many pounds around your middle, to hair loss, to high cholesterol. You name it — they have a pill for it! Smith Wigglesworth, a powerful faith healer in the late nineteenth and early twentieth centuries, said that the majority of people would lose their faith because they would too quickly utilize the medical profession to take care of their physical needs instead of relying on the Word of God. I'm not belittling the medical profession. I believe God works through these incredible men and women to help cure diseases and repair injury. But, for most people, faith in medicine is much greater than their faith in God's ability to heal them. Many do not even consider asking God for healing. Their immediate response to any ailment is to run to the medicine cabinet or consult a physician.

On top of our quick access to pills, we practice destructive habits. We eat anything and everything in front of us — slaves to our taste buds and willing accomplices to every food advertising scheme. We stay up too late and rest too little. We don't exercise and we give in to stress, anxiety and the demands of everyday life.

What I am saying is that we need to rely on God's Word. There are many Scriptures in the Bible that deal with health, healing and the physical body. There are Scriptures that help us to walk in discipline and overcome destructive habits. Health belongs to us. Our bodies are a gift from God and an invaluable resource that must be protected, taken care of and used wisely.

Social:
(Relationships)

I have seen relationships in my own family break down through offense. It happens in every family; someone gets offended and relationships are separated, causing pain and creating wounds that can last for generations. This can also happen in church families. In the area where I live, there is a certain denominational church that seems to have a church on every corner. This results from a church split. Imagine how effective they could be as a unified force. How much more effective would their influence in the community be? Even in offices it can be difficult to work with others during long periods of time. Diverse beliefs and backgrounds, different moral standards, varying work ethics and a host of other variables can make the office a hostile social environment to work in.

All relationships will experience testing at some time. Even the closest relationships built with the highest intimacy and covenant will undergo periods of stress. Building quality, enduring relationships require focus. And so we need to focus on how to have healthy social relationships with our spouse, our children, our family members, our coworkers, people in the church arena, and others. One of the greatest opportunities for success in our life is through the area of good, quality relationships. In fact, what is imparted to us and what we impart to others may be the most important aspect of fulfilling our destiny. Impartation of your knowledge, your skills, your experience

— even your anointing comes through relationship. Strong covenant relationships give you a network that is vital to your growth and potential.

When dealing with the realm of relationships, you must be able to discern which relationships in your life are healthy and which are not. You need to look for and develop the "God-relationships" that add value to your life and increase your sphere of influence and effectiveness. Relationships that drain you emotionally or limit your opportunities should be severed.

In Acts 4, there is a report given of the elders in the church. Both Peter and John had been in a situation where the Scribes and Pharisees were coming against them. It says in Acts 4:23, "And being let go, they went to their own companions..." They left the Scribes and Pharisees and returned to the people with whom they had a like-minded, precious faith with. That's what you have to do in social relationships. If you hang with people who are negative, pessimistic and filled with doubt and unbelief, you are going to be influenced by this and fall in that trap. In Ephesians 4:23 (*AMP*) it says, "And be constantly renewed in the spirit of your mind (having a fresh mental and spiritual attitude)...." This Scripture speaks not only to the soul, but also to the social arena. You must operate with an attitude of victory. You must begin the day determined not become offended. You must determine your responses of love, good reports and positive speech to those who come to you with strife, gossip or negativity. Social relationships affect our home, the marketplace and our mission field. Because of this, it is vital that we get a handle on this area and learn to function successfully.

DISC Behavioral Model

Most relationship issues arise from personality differences. In the Amplified Bible, you can see certain areas where God tells us that we must align our personality with Christ.

> "In order that you may not grow disinterested and become spiritual sluggards, but imitators, behaving as do those who through faith (by their leaning of the entire personality on God in Christ in absolute trust and confidence in His power, wisdom, and goodness) and by practice of patient endurance and waiting are now inheriting the promises."
>
> Hebrews 6:12 AMP

If you are going to focus on inheriting the promises of God, then you must align your personality with God's. To do this successfully, you must learn to identify individuals who have a different personality style than yours and then learn what to do in order to relate to them?

I am a behavioral consultant in the area of behavioral analysis using the DISC model.   It is impossible to cover the full scope of this here, but I want to give you a condensed version that will help you gain an understanding of behavioral styles. There are four different behavioral styles that I want to cover. Most personalities are a combination of two or more of these behavioral styles, but most people have one dominant style that makes up their personality.

D

The D is for those who are dominate, decisive and very task-oriented. This personality style makes up about 3% of the population. These people want things accomplished and done fast. They are direct and are self-starters. Their greatest fear is to be taken advantage of. People with this personality style are often CEO's, business owners or leaders of organizations. They are bored with details and prefer to keep their eye on the big picture and the bottom line.

- Strengths: problem solvers, risk takers, challenge the status quo, innovative

- Weaknesses: argumentative attitude, overstep authority, attempt too much at once

People with "D" Styles: Dr. Martin Luther King Jr., Richard Nixon, Donald Trump, Michael Jordan, Solomon, Nehemiah, The Apostle Paul

I

The I is for those who are influencers and are very people-oriented. This personality style makes up 11% of the population. People with this personality are enthusiastic, optimistic, persuasive, emotional and impulsive. They love to have a party and love to make things fun. Their greatest fear is rejection. People with this personality style are often great speakers and sales people and love to work with others.

- Strengths: creative problem solvers, great encouragers, peacemakers, able to motivate others

- Weaknesses: inattentive to details, does not listen attentively, prefer popularity above results, overuse of facial and hand gestures

People with "I" Style: Bill Cosby, Robin Williams, Carol Burnett, Bill Clinton, Peter, King Saul, Joshua

S

The S is for those who are stable, secure and people-oriented with those they know (relatives, friends). They are family oriented, team players, steady, predictable and friendly. This personality style makes up 69% of the population. This comprises the largest segment within our population. These people like things to be easy. They are people who like to know the schedule and prefer to be involved in things that are already established, but they do not like conflict. Their greatest fear is change. Research shows that this personality style requires a process to be in place in order for them to be successful. People with this personality style are great individuals in many areas of society and are often very loyal to organizations, churches, teams and companies.

- Strengths: reliable, dependable, loyal team workers, compliant to authority, good listeners.

- Weaknesses: resist change, hold a grudge, difficulty establishing goals or priorities, sensitive to criticism, need a process to be successful

People with "S" Style: Mister Rogers, Oprah Winfrey, Andy Griffin, Mother Teresa, Abraham, Jacob, Anna

C

The C is for those who are compliant, conscientious and very task-oriented. This personality style makes up 17% of the population. These people want things done right and they aren't going to do them over again. They take their time in order to do things with accuracy. They slow the process down for correctness and they require many facts and data to back up their decisions. Their greatest fear is criticism. People with this personality style are often engineers, accountants, in research and development or other detail oriented jobs that require a high degree of accuracy.

- Strengths: thorough in all activities, gather, test and define all information, systematic, have high standards, even tempered

- Weaknesses: Get bogged down in details, will give rather than argue, will not verbalize feelings, need a process to be successful

People with "C" Style: Tiger Woods, Jimmy Carter, Bill Gates, Mr. Spock, Luke, Mary, Ruth, Elijah

---

In most cases, you are a combination of these behavioral styles. For example, I am a personality that is an "ID" behavioral style. I am people oriented and I like to see results fast. I am decisive and goal oriented, but I also enjoy fun and love to fellowship with people. I don't like to be taken advantage of and I don't like to be rejected. Because I understand behavioral style, when I encounter people who might say something against me or take advantage of me, I know that if I will blend my personality style and behavior with theirs, I can get in sync with them and have a more fruitful relationship.

Some of the greatest issues that arise in families, in the workplace and in the church are a result of personality differences and people not being able to get in sync with each other to cooperate effectively. This always creates major issues that can lead to huge rifts and deep offenses.

When I became enlightened by this information, it changed my life. After about ten years of marriage to Cindy, I realized that I married my opposite behavioral style. During the first ten years, my focus had been to change her to be more like me, and all the while, she was trying to change me to become more like her. But as we learned about behavioral styles and discovered more about ourselves and each other, we discovered that for the most successful relationship, we must blend our personality styles. This understanding keeps me from saying things to my wife today that I would have said without hesitation earlier in our marriage. I realize that saying certain things hurts her, and so I know to keep my mouth shut. I blend my personality style, becoming more aware of others and understanding how best to communicate with them. Yes, this defies, "This is who I am — deal with it!" Blending your behavioral style takes effort on your part. This effort is often unseen and the rewards for this action will not often receive verbal praise or notice. Your reward is a healthy relationship. To have healthy social relationships you must learn when to say things, what things to say and how to say them. You must also learn what things not to say and when it is best to just hold your tongue. It is helpful to identify the areas of each individual's behavior that can hurt them the most. Success in dealing with people is increased when you know how to steer clear of their greatest fears. The 'D' gets angry when taken advantage of, the 'I' crumbles when rejected, the 'S' can't handle rapid change, and the 'C' can't take much criticism.

When my children were very young, I was able to train them up in the DISC behavioral style. My daughter was getting a "C" grade in a certain subject in high school, and I knew she was an "A" student. I set out to identify what the problem was. The teacher for this subject was very detail oriented and needed all the facts. At this time in her life, my daughter was not very detail oriented and would only list three or four facts when the teacher was looking for ten! I showed my daughter that it was in her best interest to blend her personality style, and get in sync with the teacher. I counseled her to find out what he needed and then simply do what he asked her to do. When she began to do this, she turned that grade from a "C" to an "A." Even your children can learn to blend their personality style and see success. The key to maintaining great relationships is for you to "blend" your style with others to see the best results in a relationship.

I highly recommend that you take the time and find an opportunity to become educated (or even certified) in this system. It would be very beneficial to you. A personal friend of mine, Dr. Sanford Kulkin, is the President and distributor of the DISC personality system. You can take an on-line behavioral profile to identify your style or receive training at www.discinsights.com.

Financial

Finances are an area where many, many people have major issues. Most people that I encounter are living deep in debt. They are overextended and they have no hope of digging themselves out of this situation. This limits their giving potential, robs them of their dreams, and keeps them in bondage (debt is bondage). The Bible says that we should owe no man anything except love.

I want to show you how to apply the principles of God in of your finances and help you begin to see God moving in that arena. I want to share with you some of the things that I did which brought financial increase into my life. I literally sowed my way out of poverty. Growing up, my father worked in a steel mill. Our family was smack dab in the middle class. By a miracle, I was able to get into college and graduate with a degree in Business Administration. I began working in sales and experienced some financial success. But even with more money, I realized that I was still operating with a poverty mindset. I still had a spirit of poverty on me. I needed to become educated. I listened to some audio books and some teachings from a man of God who was teaching on financial provision. I began to apply those principles.

Number One: The Tithe

I realized that I needed to bring my tithe into the house of God. This meant that I gave the first 10% of my gross income to God. I grasped an understanding that all my income belonged to God, and giving Him this tenth was my acknowledgement of my stewardship over His finances. The motivation behind this was obedience. Malachi 3:8-11 talks about the tithe. It tells us that when you bring your tithe into the store house (which is your local church where you get spiritually fed), that God will open up the windows of heaven for you and pour out a blessing so that there will not be room enough to receive it. It goes on to say that God will rebuke the devourer for you. I can testify to the truth of this Scripture. I am a man who faithfully tithes. My financial status has greatly improved because I continue to obey what God said with joy. As I give God 10%, He blesses the entire 100% and continues to bring financial increase.

Number Two: First Fruits

I gained an understanding of first fruits. From the teachings I studied, I decided to put the principle of first fruits into practice. The Bible tells me that God owns the first fruits. So when I received a raise (an increase), the very first time that this was reflected in my paycheck, I gave that entire first amount (the first fruits) to God. For example, say your paycheck is $600/wk and you receive a raise that will take you to $700/week. A first fruits offering would mean that you give that first $100 increase to God (above your normal tithe). From that time until now, any time I receive a raise or increase, I give the first fruits of that increase to God. This is also motivated from obedience. The promise of First Fruits in the Bible is that our vats would overflow with wine and our barns would also be overflowing (Proverbs 3:9-10). Whenever I give God first fruits, I experience even greater increase.

Number Three: Alms

I experienced blessing and increase both through the tithe and from first fruits giving. These are given out of an obedient heart. Alms is another type of giving, one that is motivated by compassion or sympathy. Alms is the only thing that you give to man. You give alms to men or women in need and you do it privately because the Bible tells us to do it in secret (Matthew 6:3-4). It is seeing people in need, being moved by compassion and helping them out. Giving alms is giving to the poor. God says that His response to you blessing the poor is that He will repay you. (Matthew 6:4). If I give $1,000 in alms, then God promises to return this $1,000 back to me. God is pleased when you give alms. In the Acts 10, God answers the prayers of Cornelius, telling him that the alms he had given had gone up as a memorial and a remembrance in heaven.

Number Four: Giving/Sowing

But, I realized that to receive greater financial provision, I needed to give something to God to multiply. My tithe opens the windows of heaven and rebukes the devourer. Giving first fruits causes my vats and barns to overflow. God pays me back when I give alms. But the final area of giving is seed. Seed is motivated by faith. It goes beyond addition and moves into multiplication! It is possible to sow your way out of poverty and into prosperity. You do this through seed or offerings. This is when you specifically give a seed or an offering to God, not to a man or even to a ministry even though money does go to them. You must realize that you are sowing it to God. The Bible says that if I sow a seed, He will bring forth a multiplication of that seed, 30, 60 or even 100 fold! God multiplies your seed, responds to your faith AND your stewardship to take you to the next financial level. This, coupled with discipline, can rapidly get you out of debt. Remember, the motivation behind the seed is faith. It is impossible to please God without faith. The key is to make sure that you are operating according to the faith that you have. Don't expect a $50,000 increase when you only have $5,000 faith. And don't expect anything if you are in disobedience to the tithe or you are motivated by greed. Faith for financial increase is about distribution. Increase brings great rewards, but God gives abundantly to those who have an open hand and walk in a spirit of generosity. Your faith is built every time God answers a prayer or fulfills a promise. Faith is a process of walking through. The more increase you experience, the greater your faith. The greater your faith, the more increase you will experience. There is great joy in cheerful giving. There is great reward when you see the fruit of your giving in someone's life, in the success of a cause or increase to the Kingdom of God!

Major Increase!

In my own life, when I begin to sow my seed to God, I am careful to name my seed for what I am believing for. God has always made provision for me. Why? Because He keeps His Word! It is the principles of God at work. We said in our STAND acronym, that if you will apply the principles and walk in what you have learned through revelation knowledge, God will always do His part. Your part is to bring your tithes, your first fruits, your alms and your seed offerings to God and understand that there is provision in each one of those areas. His part is to open the windows of Heaven, to rebuke the devourer from your finances, to cause your vats and your barns to overflow and to multiply your seed.

Each year, I plan my giving. I go before the Lord and ask Him to reveal what He would like me to stretch my faith for. In the year 1999, I was devising my giving plan for 2000 and I told the Lord, "I want to give you an extra $10,000 beyond what I gave last year." First, I told God I wanted to give an extra $10,000 and I released my faith for what I did not have. As I did this, my spirit was quickened and God spoke to me that it was about time that someone put a demand on Him and make a giving plan. The reason I felt God say that was because most people do not have a yearly giving plan. Do you?

Second, I determined that my plan for giving in a new year could not be less than what I gave in the previous year. I want you to understand that God has provision for you to get out of debt and become a wealth distributor in the household of God. Christians need to begin establishing wealth. Deut 8:18 tell us that we have been given the power to get wealth to establish God's covenant (found in Genesis 12:2-3) that you have been empowered to prosper to be a blessing. I prosper financially so that I can be a blessing. There are people that need a blessing. Wealth in the Kingdom is for distribution. Wealth distribution is happening throughout the earth. You see men like Bill Gates and Warren Buffet beginning to distribute their wealth to help social causes. Genesis 1:28 tells us that we are to use the resources of the earth for both God and man. I am telling you that I am using my resources right now to help God build his Kingdom and to help man. This is a great opportunity.

I told you that I entered into a covenant relationship with God, knowing that I wanted to give Him an extra $10,000. Three events took place that year that changed my life. The first happened in March. This was when we usually get our bonus for the Fortune 500 Company I worked for. This particular year, we did not make the volume number of the prior year. This means no bonus. My boss called and told me the news that there would be no bonus. I responded to him that I didn't believe this. I told my boss that I had sown the year before toward the bonus. I told him that I believed in seed time and harvest and that I had sown last year to receive this year's bonus. He laughed and reaffirmed that there would be no bonus this year. A few days later, he called me and said the company had changed their position. Not only that, but they would be issuing a bonus to me for $20,000! Here I was, believing God for an extra $10,000 to sow and in the month of March, God gave me double.

The second event that changed my life occurred when I went to a Christian convention and there was a gentleman preaching on how the blessing of God is not stuff, but rather, the blessing of God is the coat of Abraham that we wear. He explained that everything we touch turns to gold. When you put God first, He blesses everything you do. I began to make my confession that I was empowered to prosper to be a blessing. I came out of that meeting and called my boss at my corporate office. On my voice mail was a message that the company I worked for had made a lot of money and for the first time in their history, they would be issuing a second bonus of $10,000! So now I am standing there, looking up into the Heavens with an extra $30,000 in my hand, thanking God because I had promised to give Him an extra $10,000.

Well a few months later, I went to New York City for a meeting, and my boss came up to me and said that they had looked at other competitive Fortune 500 companies and with my managerial responsibilities, I was not making enough money. On their initiation, they gave me a $12,000 raise and made it retroactive for the year. So, in the course of believing God for an extra $10,000 to give Him, God brought me a $42,000 increase to my income. See how good God is! When you begin to focus and apply the principles of God, confessing the Word of God over these specific areas: spiritual, emotional, physical, social and financial, God will make provision for you.

SUMMARY

We lack revelation knowledge in each of these five areas. According to Ephesians 1:17-19, we are to pray for a spirit of wisdom and revelation. We are to ask God to enlighten the eyes of our heart and open them to know and to understand the hope of His calling and the riches of His inheritance for the saints. You have a great opportunity to ask God for revelation knowledge. I challenge you to review your Needs Assessment and ask God to show you your greatest need. Identify the specific area and we'll begin to focus on the process to bring victory for you.

FOCUS Points

A SUMMARY OF WHAT YOU HAVE LEARNED

Chapter Four Focus Points

- You must do a Needs Assessment on yourself to go to the next level.

- You operate in 5 keys areas in your life. These are the key areas where you need to stay focused on: spiritual, emotional (soul), physical, social (relationships), and financial (economic).

- Blend your personality style to get in sync with others.

- Understand the principles of how God's Kingdom works — seed time and harvest.

Chapter Five

SEED Minded vs. NEED Minded

Are you seed minded or are you need minded? To experience a focus fulfilled life, you must gain the mentality of being seed minded wherever you go. When you are in church, at work, with your family, out shopping or even on vacation, you must always be on the lookout for opportunities to sow seed. Most people operate from a need minded perspective. They are perhaps aware of their physical, emotional and financial issues, and are seeking to have their needs met. The principles of God operate in seed time and harvest (Mark 4). We need to operate in a seed time mentality. God has blessed us so that we can be a blessing to others. We are His vehicle of blessing on the earth. We must constantly look for opportunities to give seed out and bless to others.

> "And I will make of you a great nation, and I will bless you with abundant increase of favors and make your name famous and distinguished, and you will be a blessing — dispensing good to others.

"And I will bless those who bless you (who confer prosperity or happiness upon you) and curse him who curses or uses insolent language toward you; in you will all the families and kindred of the earth be blessed and by you they will bless themselves."

Genesis 12:2-3 AMP

"And God, Who provides seed for the sower and bread for eating, will also provide and multiply your resources for sowing and increase the fruits of your righteousness which manifests itself in active goodness, kindness, and charity."

2 Corinthians 9:10 AMP

God will provide seed to those who sow. Let me say that again — God WILL provide seed to those who sow. If you are need minded, then God can't multiply your resources for sowing because you are not looking to sow seed. You must become seed minded. You must begin to actively seek opportunities to sow seed. As you begin your 40 days of focus, I challenge you to sow seed every day. Sow a seed of encouragement, perform acts of kindness to strangers, or bless someone with financial provision. This could be as simple as sending an encouraging e-mail or card, or letting someone in front of you in line as you smile and say, "God bless you." This could mean that you give a server a large tip or buy a bag of groceries for a neighbor. I know of a man who went out and bought chrysanthemums for every family in his neighborhood. He put them all in a wagon and hand delivered them to each neighbor, using it as an opportunity to introduce himself and share kindness. Not long ago I was in a restaurant and gave the waitress a $100 tip. I made her day!

Sowing Seeds - examples

Once, while in another city on business, I found myself eating dinner in a high class hamburger restaurant. A group of five teenage girls came in that looked about 13 or 14 years old. I overheard that they were there celebrating one of the girl's birthdays. I was minding my business, eating my dinner and the Lord spoke to me and said, "I want you to buy dinner for those girls."

Immediately I thought to myself, "What are they going to think? You aren't some dirty old man — is this even appropriate?"

God said, "Don't say anything to them. Buy their meal, walk out and thank Me for it."

Without further hesitation, I called over their waiter, telling him that God told me to buy dinner for that table. I made sure they were all going to get ice cream or something as part of the celebration. I went further and told the waiter that not only did I want to pay for their check, but I also wanted to bless him with a big tip as well. I told him that I had been prospered by God so that I could be a blessing to both him and them. His eyes got real big. You see, I am seed minded. I want to be a blessing. I told the waiter to bring me the bill. I paid the bill and gave him $50 above the usual tip. He was all smiles as I walked out of the restaurant. Of course, I don't know the rest of the story, but I can only imagine the pleasure the waiter experienced as he informed the girls that their bill had been taken care of. He got to be part of the whole plan. And then I can imagine what the girls said to their parents about some guy in the restaurant who bought their whole meal. Only God knows what effects this act of kindness had on each of their lives, but they will all remember the event for some time to come. That's pretty awesome.

Another example. I was staying in a hotel in upstate New York, and I had some individuals coming to my hotel room to do some strategic planning. I returned to my room around 3:00 PM and found that it had not yet been cleaned

85

up from the prior night. My meeting was scheduled for 3:30, so I went into the hall, found a maid, and asked if she could possible come take care of my room really quickly so I could have it ready in time for my meeting. She was very gracious and kind, and accommodated me without hesitation or complaint. As she was finished and began walking down the hall, I gave her a $20 bill. As I left her, I heard her start thanking Jesus saying, "Thank you. Thank you, Jesus. You knew I needed this money. Oh, thank you, Lord!" And that was just twenty bucks — I should have given her a hundred! You see what happens? When we, the blessed people, become seed minded and we sow our seed, God brings more seed into our hand so we can sow it and continue to bless others.

What to Plant, What to Eat

Second Corinthians 9:10 tells us that God provides seed for sowing and bread for eating. You have to know what seed to give and what seed to eat. If you are in financial straights, you are probably consuming every dime you have to make ends meet. This means that not only are you eating the seed God gave you for bread, but you are also eating the seed that God provided for you to sow. If you aren't seed minded you are need minded. What I'm asking you to do in this next 40 days is to be in a constant period of sowing. Become seed minded. Look for an opportunity to be a blessing to somebody each day.

As I go to work every day, I am fully aware that my business is my ministry. I deal with a lot of hurting people every day, and so do you. I'm looking for ways to be a blessing to those individuals. I encourage you, as you begin to focus and prepare yourself in the next 40 days, to *sow something* into somebody each day. Be a blessing to somebody. Don't eat your seed. Allow the Spirit of God to speak to you about what you need to do. You are never without the power to give. Even if your finances are tight, you can perform acts of service, acts of kindness or speak words of encouragement. If you become seed minded and start looking for ways to bless people with what you have, God WILL begin to multiply your resources and place seed in your hand!

The First 40 Days

Focus on the Spirit ✳

In your first 40 days of focus, I want you to focus on the Holy Spirit. As I began developing *The Focus Fulfilled Life* and taking this series into churches, the Lord challenged me to have people begin to focus on the Holy Spirit for the first 40 days. Why? John 6.63 says it is the Spirit that gives life! Before you start praying for things in your spiritual growth, or for answers to weaknesses of your flesh, or to have areas in your soul renewed, or for physical needs, social relationships or financial provision, step back and focus on the greatness and the power of the Holy Spirit. You see, that is the key and the foundation for developing a focus fulfilled life. I am looking well beyond 40 days. I am talking about creating a process that will yield a lifestyle of focus. I am encouraging you to focus on a specific area in your life for 40 days out of every quarter. One 40 day period will bear fruit, but sustainable success in every area of your life will require a process that is ongoing. If you are going to commit to this process, a strong foundation that comes from focusing on the Spirit of the Most High God.

THREE KEY AREAS

"There shall come forth a Rod from the stem of Jesse,
And a Branch shall grow out of his roots.

The Spirit of the LORD shall rest upon Him,

The Spirit of wisdom and understanding,

The Spirit of counsel and might,

The Spirit of knowledge and of the fear of the LORD.

His delight is in the fear of the LORD,

And He shall not judge by the sight of His eyes,

Nor decide by the hearing of His ears;

But with righteousness He shall judge the poor,

And decide with equity for the meek of the earth;

He shall strike the earth with the rod of His mouth,

And with the breath of His lips He shall slay the wicked."

Isaiah 11:1-4 NKJV

Begin to focus on the Holy Spirit. As you do, He will give you wisdom, understanding, counsel, might, knowledge and the fear of God. And then you will have understanding and be able to rapidly respond in obedience to the Spirit of God in any area that He speaks to you about. You won't be moved by what you see or what you hear; you will be directed by the voice of God. You will be able to judge the enemy by speaking over him (Isaiah 11:4).

How do you think Jesus took on the devil when He was in the wilderness for 40 days? He spoke the Word of God to him. How do you think the earth was created in Genesis 1.3, 6, 9, 11, 14, 20, 22, 24, 26, 28, 29 - *and God said.* God spoke it. So, if God spoke and created things and if Jesus defeated enemies by the Word of His mouth, doesn't it make sense that we're going to have to do it the same way?

Key One: The Voice Behind the Word

The first key area is being able to hear the voice of the Spirit behind God's Word. This is critical. It is one thing to read the Word everyday but if you do not hear His voice behind the Word telling you what to do, it will be fruitless. There are so many distractions in this age that keep us from hearing the voice of God. I am challenging you today that you need to hear God's voice. One of the greatest examples of the power of hearing God's voice is found in the book of 2 Samuel. King David, the Bible tells us, was a man after God's own heart. God established him to be king over Israel. Throughout his life, David had developed the ability to hear God's voice.

David Becomes King

"And David perceived that the Lord had established him king over Israel and that He had exalted his kingdom for His people Israel's sake."

2 Samuel 5:12 AMP

David Asks God

"David inquired of the Lord, saying, Shall I go up against the Philistines? Will You deliver them into my hand?"

2 Samuel 5:19 AMP

See, David had to inquire of God and require God to speak to him. The first thing to do in these 40 days is to ask to hear God's voice through the Holy Spirit. Reading God's Word is rewarding, however, if you don't hear the voice *behind* God's Word, you'll never know what you have to go do. Inquire of the Lord. Ask Him to speak to you!

God Answers David

"And the Lord said to David; Go up, for I will surely deliver them into your hand."

2 Samuel 5:19 AMP

How many times do we act on things based on what we think we should do or believe should happen. How often do we make decisions that affect our lives and our future without hearing God's voice, without the wisdom of God? Is it possible that this is why we don't experience victory and success? What David did was pray through. He waited to act until he heard God's voice. He inquired of God and required God to speak to him. When he won the battle, He named the place, "Lord of breaking through."

"And David came to Baal-perazim, and he smote them there, and said, The Lord has broken through my enemies before me, like the bursting out of great waters. So he called the name of that place Baal-perazim, Lord of breaking through."

2 Samuel 5:20 AMP

After this victory, the Philistines came against David again. David knew God was with him. God had already given him instructions to fight the Philistines and they were delivered into his hand. He had experience now. He could have addressed his army with a strategy and they would have confidently followed his instructions. What did David do? He went back to God and asked Him what to do.

"When David inquired of the Lord, He said, "You shall not go up, but go around behind them and come upon them over opposite the mulberry (or balsam) trees. And when you hear the sound of marching in the tops of the mulberry trees, then bestir yourselves, for then has the Lord gone out before you to smite the army of the Philistines.

And David did as the Lord had commanded him, and smote the Philistines from Geba to Gezer."

2 Samuel 5:23–25 AMP

David heard God's voice. What he did the first time wouldn't have worked the second time. He had to inquire of the Lord EVERY time. He could not simply rely on his past experience, knowledge and skill. He needed the voice of God. It's critical to the foundation of the focus fulfilled life that you spend the first 40 days listening and gaining the ability to hear the voice of God.

How do you do that? Begin by getting into a quiet place. Remove distractions. Turn off the television, turn off the radio, the Internet, the cell phone, Blackberry, and the Instant Messenger. Find a place where you won't be interrupted and respect the presence of the Holy Spirit. Take a pen, a notebook and your Bible and get into a quiet place where you can sit down and listen. Be still. Let God speak to you. Begin to develop a listening ear so that God can speak to you.

In chapter one I shared the testimony of my covenant brother, Jim Sanderbeck. When I got the phone call that he had experienced a cardiac arrest, I immediately got on my face and prayed that God would save his life. Within three to five seconds, God spoke to me and said, "I caught

it. Stand up and begin to praise and thank Me. It's over."
I stood up immediately and told my wife to get up off the
floor, that we were going to thank God because He had
already saved Jim. I heard the voice of God tell me that it
was okay. My wife and I spent a few moments just thanking
and praising God when I got another phone call. It was
Jim's daughter, telling me everything was okay. She told
me that the doctors had caught it, and that even though
there were issues in his heart, he was alive and not dead! I
had heard God's voice and responded in obedience. Within
moments, I had confirmation that what God had told me
was the absolute truth. You CAN hear the voice of God. He
STILL speaks to us just like He did in the days of King David.

I have another example to share with you. This one
isn't about a life or death issue, but represents how much
God cares about every detail of your life. When I was
downsized from the Fortune 500 Company, I went to work
for another individual for a period of three years. In this
time, my income level dropped significantly and I really
had to rely on God for provision as I was building this new
business and this new program. On my birthday, I was
driving near a local mall and I heard God's voice speak to
me, telling me that the shirts I liked for $35, He wanted to
give me for $6.99/each. I turned my car around, and went
into JCPenny. Sure enough, there were the shirts I liked,
retail price: $35. Above the shirts was a sale sign that
said $9.99. I asked the clerk if the shirts were on sale and
she confirmed that they were on sale for $9.99. This may
sound crazy, but I knew God had told me they were $6.99,
so I asked her, "Are you sure that is the correct sales
price?" She said, "Oh yeah, I forgot to tell you that my
manager came in just before lunch and told me to knock
all the shirts down to $6.99." I was able to buy five shirts
instead of one. See how good God is? But I had to be
able to hear the voice of God, or I would have driven right
past this opportunity and missed the blessing.

Key Two: Walking in the Spirit

The second key area is walking in the Spirit. Galatians 5 tells us clearly what we need to do. Being able to walk in the Spirit is a key to success in our lives. How can we stay in the Spirit? You probably just thought about some strange individual you know that goes around all day spouting, "The Lord said...The Lord told me...I was just quickened in my spirit..." This is not what I am talking about. I operate and work in the Fortune 500 arena — I've been doing it for more than 30 years. I wouldn't get very far by being strange or making everyone uncomfortable with "spirit-speak." I am talking about WALKING in the Spirit. I am talking about living in the natural realm with a full awareness of what is occurring in the spiritual realm. Things can happen very quickly in your life that will take you out of the Spirit and energize your flesh. You have to be on guard, spiritually alert, in order to understand what it means to walk in the Spirit.

"But I say, walk and live habitually in the Holy Spirit (responsive to and controlled and guided by the Spirit); then you will certainly not gratify the cravings and desires of the flesh of human nature without God."

Galatians 5:16 AMP

What does that mean? Be responsive to the Holy Spirit. Responsive means reacting easily or readily to the Holy Spirit. Controlled means that we allow the Spirit to exercise authority over us, to direct and command us and to regulate our actions. The word guided means that we allow the Spirit to point out the way for us and keep us on a specific course. He gives us instruction and acts as our personal guide. So, if I'm going to be controlled, responsive to, guided and directed by the Spirit of God, then I've got to listen to what the Holy Spirit is saying. I want to encourage you that in the 40 days that are coming to hear the voice of God, and begin to allow the Spirit of God to control and guide you. Don't be controlled by your flesh, your emotions or your will. Instead, become responsive to, directed and guided by the Holy Spirit. It takes time. It takes practice. Don't be discouraged when you fall short — just try again. Let these first 40 days be a time of teaching and training. It is a process to develop this lifestyle so that as days, weeks and months go by, you'll be able to hear God's voice easily and quickly and be able to make the right decisions.

Key Three: Understanding the Holy Spirit's Provision

The final key area is to understand what the Holy Spirit is providing to you. The Bible says that the Holy Spirit will give you power.

3-things:

"But you shall receive power (ability, efficiency, and might) when the Holy Spirit has come upon you, and you shall be My witnesses..."

Acts 1:8 AMP

ABILITY

- The word ability simply means having what it takes to get the job done. Ability means possessing (or developing) a skill, an expertise or a talent. Ability means having the power to do something. God has given you the ability to get the job done.

94

☞ EFFICIENCY

- The word efficiency means to produce a desired outcome or effect with the minimum effort. How about working smarter, not harder?

☞ MIGHT

- Might means having the perseverance to win. It means you have superior strength and force. So, God is saying that He will give us the power of the Holy Spirit to give you the ability, efficiency and the might to get the job done.

The Holy Spirit

"But when the Comforter (Counselor, Helper, Advocate, Intercessor, Strengthener, Standby) comes, Whom I will send to you from the Father, the Spirit of Truth Who comes (proceeds) from the Father, He Himself will testify regarding Me. But you also will testify and be My witnesses, because you have been with Me from the beginning."

John 15:26-27 AMP

This Scripture gives seven characteristics of the Holy Spirit that you need to take time to identify with and meditate upon. You must understand that God wants you to have a relationship with the Holy Spirit. You must have a relationship with the Holy Spirit so you can hear the voice behind the Word of God. Only as your relationship with God is deepened can you can walk in the Spirit, being controlled by, responsive to, directed and guided by Him.

As you do this, the power of the Spirit of God comes upon you with the ability, efficiency and might to get the job done. Can you imagine what this would mean to your life if you begin to focus in the first 40 days on the power and the greatness of the Holy Spirit and begin to hear His voice? How awesome would that be? If you will focus on the Holy Spirit for the first 40 days, you will lay a tremendous foundation. You will begin to operate with the Holy Spirit as your guide. Then, as you move into your second 40 day period, you can focus on a specific area of need. Only now, you will be in tune to the voice of God. This multiplies the power of focus and increases the effectiveness. Then, as you focus on specific areas, identify Scriptures to meditate on and apply, set goals and objectives, you will now be able to clearly hear and obey the voice of God with concern to those areas. I promise that your life will never be the same!

FOCUS Points

A SUMMARY OF WHAT YOU HAVE LEARNED

Chapter Five Focus Points

- ↦ The key to success in life is to become seed minded, not need minded. You were created to fulfill the covenant of Genesis 12:2-3, that you have been empowered to prosper to be a blessing.

- ↦ The key to a focus fulfilled life is to have a relationship with the Holy Spirit.

- ↦ Three specific keys to focus on are to: hear the voice of God daily, walk in the Spirit (stay in the spirit and do not give any place to the devil), and finally, understand that God is the Provider of all blessings.

Chapter Six

WATCH OUT For These HINDRANCES

As you begin to develop a focus fulfilled life, you will experience hindrances and encounter obstacles that will try to impede your progress and diminish your achievement. I want to encourage you that it is possible to remove every hindrance and overcome every obstacle in your path. It is important to realize that hindrances will come, but you have the power to press through these and obtain victory.

The Revelation of God's Word

Hindrance 1 - not having ↑

Many people do not see the results they are believing God for because they lack the revelation of God's Word. The Bible says in Proverbs 29:18 *AMP* that, "where there is no vision (no redemptive revelation of God), the people perish." People are easily discouraged by the words of 'Doctor Drydust' or 'Sister Sickly' who prayed for something without results. Others are swayed by something they read or watched on the news. For others, one experience where God didn't show up for someone can cause them to base their faith on that experience instead of what the Word

don't other testimonies sway you

of God says. You must be completely persuaded that the Word of God is the final authority! God said it, I believe it and that settles it. Or more accurately, God said it — that settles it.

People operate at different levels of revelation based on their experience and revelation of God's Word. Unfortunately, many discredit the Word of God based on negative personal experiences. Faith begins where the will of God is known. The Bible is God's last will and testimony. He wants you to have all His promises, but they are only manifested when you gain revelation of them and obtain them. It takes time. It is a process to read the Word of God, listen to the voice of the Holy Spirit, and become educated in what the Word of God says about a situation.

The enemy's strategy is to kill, steal and destroy. But God has a strategy in the same verse to give you life abundantly. Whose strategy are you going to follow? If you have had a life full of bad experiences and blame God, then you have been walking in the strategy of the enemy. But if you realize that Satan is a liar and God's Word is true, then victory is obtained when you activate your faith and speak to the circumstances to change. It takes faith and patience to be a strong believer — wimps beware!

How do you get revelation knowledge? Get in the Word and get the Word in you. This is the only way to be successful. How much time do you spend in the Word? Are you using specific Scriptures to obtain your victory? Spend time with the Holy Spirit, and begin to ask Him to reveal the specific revelation you need to become successful. As you make time for Him and become more aware of His voice, you will begin to walk in the Spirit on a daily basis.

Another way to gain revelation through listening to teaching tapes or CD's and by reading books written by men and women of God that can provide insight for you into the revelation of God's Word. You will find that others have experienced the same struggles you are facing and found a way to overcome them. You can take great leaps ahead if you are willing to gain insight from the experience of others. Build on what they know and go to the next level.

Operate in God's System

hindrance (2)

Another area that creates potential hindrances comes from operating in the world's system and not in God's system. For example, take a computer that is functioning with Windows 95 as its operating system. Now, try to install new software on that computer that was designed to function with Windows XP as its operating system. No matter how great the software is, it will NEVER function properly outside of the operating system it was designed for. You were designed to function in God's system. You are fearfully and wonderfully made. But no matter how wonderful your design and how amazing your purpose, if you try to function inside the world's operating system, you will experience frustration and failure. It is a system problem! People living in the world's system will get the world's results. But living in God's system and applying His principles will produce the best results. Revelation 18:3-4 is talking to the people of God. It commands them to come out of that system!

What system? What is the world's system? One example is the world's system of debt. The average person owes between $8,000 and $10,000 in credit card debt. The Bible says in Romans 13:8 that we are to owe no man anything except to love him. Debt is bondage. When you are in debt, you are not free to obey God, you are a servant to your lender (Proverbs 22:7), you have become trapped in the world's system.

Another example is the world's system of oppression. Oppression causes a feeling of being controlled or weighed down. Oppression stifles your activity and keeps you from your God-given destiny. Oppression is tyranny, domination and coercion. It is in direct contradiction to the will of God at work in your life. The Bible says in Isaiah 54:14 that if you are established in God's system (His Kingdom which is righteousness, peace and joy in the Holy Ghost), then oppression is far from you. Are you walking in righteousness or are you still in familiar sin? Familiar sin is those areas that you try to get victory over but it continues to be a struggle. It is like killing your old man or flesh, burying him in a grave, and then, two weeks later digging him back up so you can keep doing the same old sin again. Are you living in peace and free from anxiety or are you living in fear or fighting depression?

God's system is operating when you show forth the joy of the Lord. God's system is operating when you are listening to the Holy Spirit. God's system is certainly operating when you are walking in the Spirit daily (controlled by, responsive to and directed by the Spirit —Galatians 5:16). God's operating system has your success in mind. You were born into the world's system and your old nature is comfortable there. To function in God's system will take education, training and practice. Just like it takes training to go to college and get equipped or get training in your job, you have to invest in yourself and get the equipping and training you need. Study to show yourself approved. Invest in yourself by going to conferences. Learn how the system operates and how to receive the promises of God from it.

God's financial system is seed time and harvest time (Mark 4). How do you operate in God's financial system? You need to begin to study Mark 4 and gain knowledge and wisdom about how to get out of debt and have your needs met. You need to gain an understanding of sowing financial seed. Your living is based on your giving! Listen to God's voice before you do anything and follow Him. When making major financial decisions, seek the counsel of godly men and women who have proven themselves faithful and knowledgeable in the area of finance. If you need help creating a strategy to reduce debt, then get it! There was a time when I was going to buy a new Ford Explorer. I had the plan to be out of debt in two years, so we went ahead and ordered the SUV. However, about an hour after my wife placed the call to order the truck, the Spirit of God spoke to me and told me to cancel the order. I went to my wife and told her I did not have the peace of God on this and that we needed to cancel it — which she did immediately. Only three weeks later, I was downsized by the Fortune 500 Company I was working for. I was living in God's system. God protected me. I heard His voice, obeyed it and was protected from entering a debt I would have been unable to pay.

Know Your Provider

(3) hindrance 3 is not 5

The third area of hindrance is created by not knowing who your Provider is. Your employer is just your seed sack. This is one channel God uses to provide seed for you to sow. He is your Provider, not the job! You need to know that God always brings provision to meet any need.

I love the Names of God. In every one of His names, a need is met! Below is a list of the names of God and the needs that each name meets:

☞ Jehovah

- Jehovah is derived from the Hebrew word chavah, which means life. Jehovah is literally full of life! *Exodus 6:3, Exodus 17:15, Psalm 83:18*

⌐ El Elyon

- If you have a situation that is too big and high for you then call upon the Most High God, He is El Elyon. *Genesis 14:18, Psalm 57:2, and Psalm 91:1*

⌐ El Shaddai

- If you are fighting a powerful foe, then call upon Almighty, all-powerful, whose power no foe can withstand God, He is El Shaddai. *Genesis 17:1, Genesis 28:1-3, Psalm 91:1*

⌐ Jehovah Jireh

- If you have any need for provision, then He is Jehovah-Jireh, our Provider. *Genesis 22:14, Psalm 78:20, Psalm 105:37*

⌐ Jehovah Rapha

- If you need to be healed, mended, repaired and restored, He is Jehovah Ropha, the Lord who heals us. *Exodus 15:22, Psalm 103:1-3, Jeremiah 30:17*

⌐ Jehovah Shalom

- If you need wholeness — nothing missing, nothing broken in your life, then He is Jehovah Shalom, the God of our peace. *Judges 6:24, Jeremiah 29:11, Philippians 4:7*

⌇ Jehova Rohi

- If you need someone to lead you in the right direction, He is Jehovah Rohi, our Great Shepherd. *Psalm 23, Hebrews 13:20-21, John 10:14-16*

⌇ Jehova Tsidkenu

- If you want to live in uprightness, He is Jehovah Tsidkenu, our righteousness. *Jeremiah 23:5-6, 2 Corinthians 5:21, Romans 6:17-18*

⌇ Jehova M'Kaddesh

- If you need to be cleansed and sanctified then He is Jehovah M'Kaddesh, our Sanctifier. *Leviticus 20:7-8, Isaiah 44:6, 1 Corinthians 1:30*

⌇ Jehovah Shammah

- If you need someone to be near you as you go through a battle, then He is Jehovah Shammah, the Lord who is here for you. *Exodus 25:8, Ezekiel 48:35, 2 Corinthians 6:16*

⌇ Jehovah Sabaoth

- If you need someone to fight for you during a battle, He is Jehovah Sabaoth, the Lord of Hosts. *Psalm 46:7, Isaiah 6:3, James 5:4*

☛ Jehovah Gmolah

- If you need God to recompense you (meaning to repay, to reward, or to compensate you for a loss), He will do it. *Proverbs 20:22, Jeremiah 51:56, Hebrews 10:30*

For every need you have, God is the Provider. Your provision for every situation is in His name. I said before that you have to become seed minded not need minded on a daily basis. In God's system you look to sow into others. In the world's system you look for what others owe you.

In 2 Chronicles 20, King Jehoshaphat was surrounded by his enemies. He had no way out. BUT - he could call on the Name of God!

"If, when evil comes upon us (evil is death or the curse) as the sword (Satan trying to devour you), judgment (the consequences of sin), pestilence (sickness or oppression) or famine (financial lack), we stand before this house and in thy presence, (for thy name is in this house,) and cry unto thee in our affliction, then thou will hear and help us."

2 Chronicles 20:9 AMP

The end of this story is awesome. When they called upon the Name for provision, God routed the enemies and they gathered in the spoils which took three days to bring in! They called that place the Valley of *Beracah* — the Valley of Blessing (verse 26). You see, your blessing is knowing and calling upon the Names of God. The Name *always* brings provision!

Take Personal Responsibility

(4) hindrance

   The fourth area of hindrance is created by a lack of personal responsibility. People who are not doers of God's Word do not take responsibility for their actions. The world's system has produced a generation of victims who blame all excess, deviance, aggression and shortcomings on other people and circumstances outside of their control. James 1:22 says to be doers of the Word and not merely listeners. This means that you have to obey the message. It is amazing to see the different generations that are in the world today who do not make a total commitment to the Kingdom of God. Abusive parenting or an absentee father is an excuse for the inability to commit to a marriage or even to a local church. Poverty or culture is an excuse for being habitually late — and we wonder why we are not blessed! God shows Himself strong to those who are committed to Him. He is pleased when you take responsibility to be committed to Him. You draw near to God first and *then* He draws near to you (James 4:8). I have been a leader training others in churches for over 25 years and the number one problem keeping people from reaping their harvest is laziness.

   First, they refuse to discover God's will for their own life. They want to be told what to do. God has gifted every one of us with gifts and callings, yet we are wait for a pastor or minister to hold our hand and tell us what to do. Second, once they have been told what to do, it requires effort, so they put it off until later. God once told me, "I have given you gifts, and just as you expect a broker to make money for you when you give them an investment, I also am expecting a return on My investment into you!" Wow! God wants a return on His investment. He is not pleased by a slacker (Matthew 25:14-19).

Many of you have been instructed by a man or woman of God to move into leadership training or to begin using your gifts and you have not taken responsibility to stir yourself up and become a doer! I had a couple tell me that God spoke to them ten years ago about becoming leaders and they are just stepping out now. I wanted to ask them if God was still speaking to them after ten years of disobedience! Please hear my heart; I am not trying to condemn, and I understand that it takes a lot for some people to overcome fear and obey God. But it is time for you to become a doer of what God has told you to do. You might be unsure of your gifting. If this is the case, I encourage you to go to your pastor or minister and ask to take a spiritual gifting profile. If they have not utilized this tool before, encourage them to visit buildingchurch.net, giftquestinc.com, or some other source to obtain this powerful tool. Find out what you are good at and go do it! Take the responsibility of using the gifts God has equipped you with and show God you can provide Him with a big return on His greatest investment — you!

Have Faith

(5) hindrance

The fifth area of hindrance is created by fear which is caused by unbelief. Fear produces anxiety. It results in a loss of courage and fosters apprehensive concern. Fear is the opposite of faith. Many people have a fear of failure. They fear sowing, using their gifts, rejection, not receiving after they give, fear of the unknown, etc. In fact, I have encountered people who even have a fear of success. God has given them a business or a ministry yet they won't expand it! They are afraid they can't handle the burden, worried that it will take too much time and energy. God is a God of increase and multiplication. In Genesis 1:28, God instructs us to take dominion over the earth, and to be fruitful and multiply it. He NEVER told us to be in decrease mode. If God has made provision for you, then God can help you take it to the next level of success.

> "The blessing of the LORD makes one rich, And He adds no sorrow with it."
>
> Proberbs 10:22 NKJV

After the 9/11 terrorist attacks, the enemy has increased the use of fear to paralyze and hinder people. God has not given us a spirit of fear, but a spirit of power, of love and of a sound mind (2 Timothy 1:7). He has given us a calm and well-balanced mind. The only fear we need to have is a fear of God, which is a profound reverence and awe towards Him.

Walk in Excellence

(6)hindrance

The final area of hindrance is caused by familiarity and accepting average as a standard. We have become comfortable living below the bar. That old limbo song says, "How low can you go?" Satan has lowered the bar time and again and the church responds by bending over backwards. She SHOULD take the bar and crack it across the head of the enemy, lift up the standard of Christ and take her place! We must set the standard high in the ways and purposes of God. Familiarity with the world causes us to feel good by comparing ourselves to them. We should never settle for less than excellent. We must live and walk above the norm and *way* above average. Jesus did not pay the ultimate price for us so we could live our lives in poverty and defeat. Poverty is the product of the curse, yes! not the blessing! Jesus did not say He was coming back for a defeated and worn out church, but for a glorious bride who rules and reigns this earth. The first thing God gave

man (Genesis 1:26) was dominion. He told man to subdue the earth (or to bring it under our control and under our subjection) and use its vast resources for the good of God and man. Step out of familiarity and possess your inheritance. You have been empowered to prosper to be a blessing to all mankind to shine forth the love of Jesus Christ.

In the next chapter we will begin to review the process of living a Focus Fulfilled Life. As you begin the process, please be aware that these hindrances will try to stop you and keep you from entering into great success in the Kingdom of God. Be prepared. Be on your guard. You have everything you need to overcome these obstacles and enter into victory!

FOCUS Points

A SUMMARY OF WHAT YOU HAVE LEARNED

Chapter Six Focus Points

- ↝ You must realize that Satan will try to hinder you and retain you in the same place.

- ↝ The Holy Spirit can speak to you through the Word of God to help you get revelation knowledge, understand how to operate in God's system and know who your Provider is by spending time with Him daily.

- ↝ You must take personal responsibility for your actions, walk daily in faith and expectation and do all things in a spirit of excellence.

"A lack of focus
is why many people fail.
Your focus determines
your destiny."

- John P. Kelly

Chapter Seven

The PROCESS of a FOCUS FULFILLED LIFESTYLE

OGSM Model and Planning Template

As you gain an understanding of the power of living a focus fulfilled life, we need to review the process that you will implement on a daily basis. The process is straightforward. If you will put this plan in action, you will begin to see results!

1 Make a total commitment to stay focused on specific key areas in your life: spiritual, social, relational, physical or financial.

The key is to continue the process, and even if you miss a day or two, don't give up or feel the need to start over again. There will be days when work or family objectives will keep you from your focus, but the main objective is to remain as focused as possible over a 40 day period and not quit.

"Roll your works upon the Lord (commit and trust them wholly to Him: He will cause your thoughts to become agreeable to His will and) so shall your plans be established and succeed."

Proverbs 16:3 AMP

2 Identify specific objectives that you want to obtain.

We all have blind spots (areas in which other people see a weakness, but we do not recognize), but most of us have some idea of what we need to work on in our lives. Begin to think about certain objectives that relate to the five key areas we discussed: spiritual, soul/emotional, physical, social/relational, and financial/economic. Take the time to pray and seek the Lord. Ask Him to help you articulate the objectives you want to accomplish.

"A man's heart plans his way but the Lord directs his steps."

Proverbs 16:9 NKJV

3 Set goals that are measurable and attainable.

The reason you need to set goals is because your goals propel you forward to action. Goals give you a sense of purpose and reveal your full potential. Goals give you direction and a course of action. This resolves indecision and helps you stay on a course that is headed for success. Many have dreams that they will never realize. Why? No goals. Mark Gorman says that a goal is a dream with a deadline. Set goals.

> "Commit your way to the Lord [roll and repose each care of your load on Him]; trust (lean on, rely on, and be confident) also in Him and He will bring it to pass."
>
> Psalms 37:5 AMP

4 Incorporate strategies that include: confessing specific Scriptures, identifying specific actions necessary to achieve your objectives and see results.

The key to meeting your objectives is having the right strategies in place to accomplish each element of the objective and be able to reach your goal. Nothing is more frustrating than working without a strategy or working with an unproductive or poorly planned strategy. In business, in science and in the military, significant resources and time are dedicated to developing effective strategies. Therefore, take your time and allow God to speak to you to give you the best strategies to accomplish your goals and objectives. Talk the strategy over with your accountability partner and get counsel.

> "Without counsel, plans go awry, but in the multitude of counselors they are established.
>
> Proverbs 15:22 NKJV

5 Execute the strategies daily.

Stay focused until you achieve your results. DO NOT GIVE UP — stay focused.

"...having done all the crisis demands, stand firmly
in your place. Stand therefore hold your ground,
...to that end keep alert and watch with strong
purpose and perseverance..."

Ephesians 6:13-18 AMP

6 Capture your results.

It is important to evaluate what went right and what
went wrong. When you capture your results, you gain key
learnings that will help you as you begin your next 40 day
focus.

7 Testify about your results. Give glory and thanksgiving to God.

When you testify, it builds your faith and stirs faith
in others. As you rehearse your success, you will be
encouraged and find positive momentum in your life. Above
all, give thanks to God and acknowledge His blessing in your
life at every opportunity.

"For this I will give thanks and extol You, O Lord,
among the nations; I will sing praises to
Your name."

2 Samuel 22:50 AMP

Let's begin by identifying how to execute your plan for 40 days of focus. This begins by following an OGSM model. OGSM stands for Objectives, Goals, Strategies, and Measures. In over thirty years in business and ministry, my experience has shown this to be a more focused strategic process to plan, execute, and achieve objectives. Let's look closer at this plan:

OBJECTIVES

- An objective is something that your efforts or actions are directed toward to accomplish. It is your target. It is what you aim for and the end result of your actions. This is the big picture. What are you going to focus your efforts on and what are you trying to achieve? *It is important that you write this down in words that are specific and easy to understand.*

GOALS

- We will define goals as the bite-sized pieces of your objective. Goals must keep you pointed in the direction of your main objective. What is the specific end or target you are trying to achieve? *Goals must be stated in specific numbers and should always relate to achieving your stated objectives.*

STRATEGIES

- A strategy is defined as a careful plan or method to achieve your objectives and goals. How will you get it done? What is the plan that you need to have to achieve your goals in 40 days? In this model, you will use your personal experiences (what worked and didn't work for you in the past) and you will hear the voice of God and allow Him to provide strategies for your success. *It is essential to your success that you express these strategies into words and write them down.*

⊶ MEASURES

- A measure is defined as a basis or standard of comparison. Have you achieved what you set out to do? Your measures give you a comparison of what you set out to achieve and the final results you attained. It is an important evaluation tool that helps you measure success as well as determine what areas still need work. *Measures (like goals) are stated in numbers.*

What Have You Learned

At this time, I ask you to review what you have learned in the previous chapters. Review the acronyms for FOCUS and STAND. Evaluate whether you are need minded or seed minded and review the hindrances that keep you from your focus. Most importantly, look over your Needs Assessment and pay close attention to areas where you have experienced success and areas where you saw failure. It is important to review this so that as you begin to list new strategies, you don't establish plans that have not proven successful in the past. Remember one definition of insanity is to do the same thing over and over and expect different results. The OGSM model is designed to break the cycle of repeated failure and develop a process for you to keep specific objectives and goals in front of you on a daily basis.

Purpose
The OGSM model is designed to help you apply the strategies that you receive from God as you spend time in His Word and in His presence to your life. By using this model, you will focus your drive and attention on God's Word and apply His principles to your objectives to gain success. You will be able to measure your goals as you meet your objectives and testify about God's faithfulness.

OGSM MODEL - 40 Days of Focus

On the following page, I have prepared a template on what the OGSM model looks like. As you continue reading, I have given more specific examples that can help you verbalize your own Objectives, Goals, Strategies and Measures. The examples cover the five key areas of focus - Spiritual, Physical, Emotional/Soul, Social/Relational, and Financial/Economic. You can create your own chart by following this example. First, you begin by listing your Desired Outcome. Then you will determine the OGSM.

Desired Outcome: *List your desired outcomes for the next 40 days. This will be determined by the results of your Needs Assessment.*

OBJECTIVES	GOALS	STRATEGIES	MEASURES
What are you trying to achieve?	What is your target in numbers?	How will you get it done?	Did you achieve your results?
List a **spiritual** objective.	List **spiritual** goals.	List God given strategies to reach your **spiritual** objective.	List results as God manifests your **spiritual** objectives.
List a **physical** objective.	List **physical** goals.	List God given strategies to reach your **physical** objective.	List results as God manifests your **physical** objectives .
List an **emotional or soul** (change in emotions, will, intellect) objective.	List **emotional or soul** goals.	List God given strategies to reach your **emotional or soul** objective.	List results as God manifests your **emotional or soul** objectives.

OBJECTIVES	GOALS	STRATEGIES	MEASURES
List a *social or relational* objective.	List *social or relational* goals.	List God given strategies to reach your *social or relational* objective.	List results as God manifests your *social or relational* objectives.
List a *financial or economic* objective.	List *financial or economic* goals.	List God given strategies to reach your *financial or economic* objective.	List results as God manifests your *financial or economic* objectives.

List of OGSM'S Examples

Below are some examples from each of the five key areas we have discussed. These will be helpful to you for review as you begin to identify your own Objectives, Goals and Strategies for your 40 Days of Focus.

Spiritual Examples

Spiritual Objectives: examples in this area may include: going to a higher level of spiritual growth, greater discipline in prayer, Bible reading and a consistent quiet time, spending time listening to hear the voice of God, obeying the Spirit of God diligently, taking on-line classes or Bible college courses, utilizing my gifting (such as intercession/prayer, leadership, evangelism, worship/choir, helps, healing, administration, giving, Christian education, teaching, visitation, children, youth, counseling, or service/care opportunities).

Spiritual Goals: to reach my objective of _____ _____ I will make my quiet time my number one priority, I will set aside specific timeframes to pray by getting up early in the morning, or I can set aside specific

times to pray during the day. Or, I will enroll in_____
_____ to increase my understanding of_____
_____.

Spiritual Strategies: I will identify specific Scriptures that pertain to spiritual growth, write them down and confess them during the day, get involved in meeting with a small group for prayer and fellowship, read Scriptures and mediate on them daily, determine what my gift is through a spiritual gifting profile and then meet with my pastor/minister to discuss where I fit in the church, ask the Lord to show me how my gift can impact the world and ask for influence where I work and spend time with people who do not know the Lord as Savior.

Emotional/Soul Examples

Emotional/Soul Objectives: examples of this area may include: getting on a schedule to better manage my time, controlling my emotions, gaining victory over weaknesses of my flesh (such as pride, arrogance, doubt, unbelief, fear, frustration, lust), or, letting go of my will and desires and taking up God's will for my life, obeying what God has told me to do.

Emotional/Soul Goals: to reach my objective of ___
_____ , I will ask friends if they are seeing a difference in my life after I begin to focus on these objectives, I will pay close attention to _____ and ask the Holy Spirit to make me aware each time I begin to falter in this area; I will look to see what is feeding this behavior in me (certain movies, music, friends, habits) and eliminate them from my life.

Emotional/Soul Strategies: I will spend time focusing on specific Scriptures that can help me overcome my weaknesses, I will find someone to e-mail or call me daily to encourage me to stay on fire for God and hold me accountable, I will take a behavioral style profile to learn about and understand my strengths and weaknesses.

Physical Examples

Physical Objectives: examples of this area may include: diet, weight loss, exercise, seeing a nutritionist, eating right, fasting, walking in total wholeness, getting the proper rest.

Physical Goals: to reach my objective of_____ I determine to get 7 hours of rest per night, or identify a specific calorie intake per day (1,500), or identify specific days (3-5) per week to exercise, or fast at least one day per week.

Physical Strategies: I will ride a bike, walk, swim, run, join a gym, get a personal trainer once or twice a week, enroll in a specific diet program, write down and keep track what I eat daily, identify and pray specific Scriptures over my body to be renewed like that of an eagle (Psalm 103:5).

Social/Relationship Examples

Social/Relationships Objectives: examples of this area may include: blending my personality style to improve current relationships that are not healthy, identifying what others around me enjoy and being a blessing to them, spending time with spouse and children, entering into fellowship with like-minded people, getting along better with people at work, church or any organization I am affiliated with.

Social/Relationship Goals: To meet my objective of _____ I can identify a specific number of people that you want to improve relationship with or focus on a specific number of things to do to bless your spouse or children.

Social/Relationships Strategies: I will identify and pray specific Scriptures over attaining pure and blessed relationships, I will not allow offense in my life, I refuse to hold a grudge, I will ask for forgiveness from _____ about _____. I will be the first one to apologize; I will plan to take my spouse out once a week on a date; I will pay attention to what my (spouse, children, family friends) finds important and show value to them in this area; I will spend quality time with spouse, children, family and friends; I will be a blessing to others.

Financial/Economic Examples

Financial/Economic Objectives: examples of this area may include: reducing credit card spending, working to become debt free, start a savings program, setting a budget and staying within my budget, creating a plan for purchasing a new car, house or college, use my resources to increase my influence in the workplace, start a class or discussion group finances at my workplace (bring Biblical principles into the study), start a new business, or get a creative idea from God to become a wealth distributor to build the Kingdom of God.

Financial/Economic Goals: To meet my objectives, I will sow $_____and expect a harvest of $_____, or I will focus on getting out of debt in____year(s), I will save $____to put towards a specific purchase and not borrow any money, or I will schedule____interview(s) each month to obtain a better job.

Financial/Economic Strategies: I will write down and confess financial Scriptures over my finances. I will save and purchase without credit card debt. I will enroll in a financial class and learn how to (operate on a budget, invest, estate planning, etc.). I will go back to school to earn a degree for a new job or advancement at my current employer; I will seek to gain influence within my workplace by praying for specific people and their needs (I could ask my boss for permission to start a program to meet these needs); I will get training on how to become a wealth builder and wealth distributor to build the Kingdom of God. *As you develop your financial strategies, I highly recommend that you visit* *www.icwbf.com. This is the website for the International Christian WealthBuilders Foundation where you can information and training in your finances and learn how to become a wealth builder to advance the Kingdom of God.*

Below is an example of a completed OGSM model using each of the five key areas. Again, I want to emphasize that the key to a successful OGSM plan is the preparation time you put into it *before* writing down your objectives, goals and strategies. This should not be done on impulse. I suggest that you take at least five to seven days and spend time with the Lord, fasting and asking Him what are the key objectives, goals and strategies you need to focus on in the next 40 days.

I am working to help you develop a process that you can use every quarter of the year. That means that in each quarter (90 days), you will be focusing for 40 of those 90 days on specific key objectives. You might want to put a focus on each key area for ten days. In others words, you could take the first 10 days and focus on a spiritual area, then in the next 10 days, you would focus on a soul/emotional objective and so on until the 40 days are up. What's important is finding the process that works best for you and then to stay with it. If you can start this process and implement it, in one year you *will* see greater results. Why? Because, you will have remained focused for almost half of the year on achieving specific results.

You may prefer to stay focused on only one or two critical objectives and goals and just keep the process going for each of the 40 day cycles. In other words, you will focus on one or two objectives for an entire 40 Day period and then begin a new focus on new objectives or goals in the next 40 Days. Or, you may even decide to continue on the objectives you were focusing on until you get the fullness of the manifestation you were seeking.

OGSM MODEL EXAMPLE - 40 Days of Focus

Desired Outcome: *My desire outcome is to stay focused and see the results of my OGSM plan listed below.*

OBJECTIVE	GOAL	STRATEGY	MEASURE
Spiritual I will go to a higher level spiritually in the next 40 days. I will hear the voice of God on a daily basis and be obedient to it to fulfill God's destiny for my life.	Spend __ hours a day with the Lord praying and listening to the Holy Spirit. Read__ chapters of my Bible on a daily bases. Pray for___ minutes/hours per day.	Develop a prayer and confession list that is focused on my spiritual growth. Get alone in a quiet place daily and write down what God is telling me to do. I will focus on my destiny from by mediating on what God has already spoken to me and what others have spoken to me.	Document weekly time spent with the Lord and the fruit of mylabor. Have my pastor and a covenant friend hold me accountable.
Emotional/Soul I will focus on a weak area of my life.	I will ask ___ friends about my weak area and how it affects them.	I will ask the Lord to identify a particular weakness and apply specific Scriptures to this weakness.	Did I see this weakness turn into strength? Have my pastor and a covenant friend hold me accountable.
Physical I will work out three days a week for the next 40 days. I will focus on eating right in the next 40 days.	I will spend a minimum of___ minutes working out each day of training. I will only eat ⎯⎯ calories per day for the next 40 days.	I will go to the YMCA and get a personal trainer for one day per week to help me get started and hold me accountable. I will discuss my diet with a nutritionist.	Do I feel better? Have I lost weight? Have a trainer or friend hold me accountable.

OBJECTIVE	GOAL	STRATEGY	MEASURE
Social/ Relationship I will develop a closer relationship with my spouse and children. I will develop covenant relationships with key individuals of like precious faith.	I will spend ___ hours per week focusing on a closer relationship with my spouse and children.	Identify key areas that my spouse and my children like and sow into those areas. I will spend time teaching and training my children in the ways of God and spend time in prayer with my spouse and children.	Are my relationships improving? Did I spend time sowing into my children? Have my pastor and/or a covenant friend hold me accountable.
Financial/ Economic I will become a person of influence within my workplace and see advancement and increase. I will pray to be debt free.	I will pray for $__ or__% of increase to come to me within the next timeframe. I will reduce my debt to $___in timeframe.	Develop a prayer and confession list that is focused on financial provision and increase. I will serve God in my workplace with joy and honor. I will not use my credit card and wait on purchases until I have the money.	Have I seen increase and favor come my way? Is my debt starting to be reduced? Have my pastor and/or a covenant friend hold me accountable.

The process for creating and following your own personal OGSM plan is developed for you in the Focus Fulfilled Life Workbook. You can use the examples in this chapter to create your own, or you can take advantage of the Focus Fulfilled Life Workbook to help you achieve even greater success. The Workbook guides you as you focus on a particular area. It is filled with 40 Scriptures for each of the five key areas as well as specific confessions for each area, encouragement, daily reviews and other helpful tools to guide you through the process of creating a Focus Fulfilled Life!

FOCUS Points

A SUMMARY OF WHAT YOU HAVE LEARNED

Chapter Seven Focus Points

- ☞ You must spend time alone with God to hear God's voice in preparation of developing an effective OGSM plan.

- ☞ Set reasonable goals. Each objective and goal must be within reach for you to attain.

- ☞ God is a God of strategy. As Jesus only did what He heard the Father say to do, you can also begin to utilize the strategy that God provides when you spend the time with Him.

Chapter Eight

EXECUTION and RESULTS

The second process that will help you achieve a focus fulfilled lifestyle is an Execution Goal Chart. This chart will help keep you focused on the specific tasks and strategies you need to perform in order to reach you goals. Keep this chart with you during the day or tuck it inside your Bible. Use it to help keep you focused and make sure you meet your time targets. It is critical to put a date on each objective and goal, this will help you remain focused and achieve greater results.

Execution

Execution means to fully carry out a plan or action. In other words, execution is the process to make things happen. Lack of execution is the major cause of failure in businesses, organizations, and even in personal lives. This process of using an Execution Goal Chart has been effective in my own personal, business and church life to help individuals focus on executing their OGSM's and achieving greater success.

What are the reasons why people do not stay focused and do not see greater results? Let take a look.

- **Personality**

  - According to statistics, only 3% of the population possess the DNA to set goals on their own and get the job done. That means that in order for the other 97% to be successful, they need to create a process to follow that will help them to set goals and follow a course of action so they can begin to see the success they have been dreaming of.

- **History**

  - Focusing on past failures and why you did not achieve a specific goal or objective can sabotage your future. The Apostle Paul tells us in Philippians 3:13, *"Forget those things which are behind (past), and reach forth for those things that are before you.* You cannot allow your history to determine your future, press forward and you will receive the prize of the high calling of God (Philippians 3:14).

- **Priority**

  - Lack of focus or not placing a high priority on a project can make it ineffective. Behaviorally speaking, over 69% of the population have difficulty prioritizing effectively. *The Focus Fulfilled Life* provides a process that will help you identify and establish priorities and follow through with a course of action to see results.

- **Perseverance**

  - To successfully execute your action plan, you must be willing to pay the price to reach your objective. Many individuals lack this drive and give up as soon as the pursuit becomes uncomfortable or difficult. You must be in *"in it to win it"* if you are going to see results.

⚷ Familiarity

- You are comfortable with your habits and routines. To succeed, you must break the familiarity of what you know and have experienced to abandon status quo. Doing a new thing requires new habits and new disciplines. Forsake the "same old, same old" mentality and begin to see what you can when you do it through Christ!

My Action Plan

How will you execute the OGSM model? The attached Goal Chart Execution Chart is a way to focus on your goals and objectives by listing the task, potential resources, strategic action plan and a completion date. This process will keep you focused and accountable to accomplish your objectives.

Lack of execution is one of the main reasons why individuals, businesses and organizations fail. Many books have been written by top professionals who feel that execution is lacking in the lives of Americans. I am a man who can execute. I have been told by my managers and peers, that I am one of the best executors in the country. I carry out the plans my company gives me with great success. Why? Because I have created a process to follow that provides for success. I have implemented these processes in all areas of my life – spiritual, emotional, physical, social and financial. I use these processes to affect my personal life, business, church and involvement in outside organizations. By execution, I mean the process of performing an effective action. Execution means to create or to produce in accordance with an idea, blueprint or plan. I have listed below an example of how you will need to fill out the Execution Goal Chart and begin to see greater success and results.

129

GOAL CHART EXAMPLE

TASKS	POTENTIAL RESOURCES	STRATEGIC PLAN	COMPLETION DATE	✓
List tasks to do daily. These tasks should stay inside your area of focus: spiritual, emotional, physical, social, or financial.	List (spiritual, emotional, physical, social or financial) resources.	List your (spiritual, emotional, physical, social or financial) strategic plan.	Assign a date to complete the task.	Check when completed. This creates account- ability and helps you measure results.

"Write the vision and engrave it so plainly upon tablets that everyone who passes may be able to read it easily and quickly as he hastens by. For the vision (your goals and objectives) is yet for an appointed time and it hastens to the end fulfillment; it will not deceive or disappoint. Though it tarry, wait earnestly for it, because it will surely come; it will not be behindhand on its appointed day."

Habakkuk 2:2-3 AMP

In other words, you need to **write down what you are focused on.** Make your focus plain and easy to follow. Then, stay focused and follow your plan so you will see the fulfillment of your objectives.

Lets look at each element of the Execution Goal Chart.

Tasks

A task is an assigned piece of work that needs to be finished within a certain time. Those with a people oriented behavioral style, must FOCUS on becoming more disciplined if they are to stay on the task and complete it. For these people, tasks are easily set aside to socialize with people. They are easily distracted by the doorbell, telephone or email message. If your goal is to spend one hour in fellowship with the Lord each day, then this would appear in the TASK box of your Execution Goal Chart. Whatever task you need to do should appear in a separate section of the TASK box so that you can see it every day. This will help you focus on the task and become a doer of it.

> "But be doers of the Word, and not hearers only, deceiving yourselves."
>
> James 1:22 NKJV

Potential Resources

A resource is a source of supply or support. In this box, list those people who will hold you accountable. Also list any other information or support you can gather to make your objectives and goals a reality. No man is an island. You need others. The greatest growth I ever experienced came through involvement in a small group as I was held accountable by the leader and other like-minded friends. When my wife and I led a small group in our home (it grew to over 50 people), we focused on equipping and training people to go to the next level, but gave them the support and held them accountable to become successful.

Strategic Plan

Strategy is defined as a careful plan or method to accomplish a goal. A plan is defined as a detailed method to achieve an end. In this section, list specific strategies you need to keep in front of you to achieve your goals and objectives. Again, I encourage you to spend time listening to the voice of God and use His strategies and the strategies you receive from the wise counsel of others. Having the right strategies and being patient to follow through will yield results!

Completion Date

To complete something means to fully carry it out to see the results. Many fall short of completion. After reaching 75 or 85% of the goal, they get bored and move on to something new. This results in unfinished projects and "almost" character. Nothing is more satisfying that being able to set your mind and heart on an objective and goal and see the results all the way to the end. Press through and cross the finish line. Your efforts will be rewarded.

On the following page there is an example of an Execution Goal Chart in process.

GOAL CHART

TASKS	POTENTIAL RESOURCES	STRATEGIC PLAN	COMPLETION DATE	✓
Spiritual Tasks: I will pray and read the Bible one hour per day to clearly hear the voice of God. I will confess 3 Scriptures, 3 times per day on God's favor over my life.	- Bible Concordance - Book or CD on God's Favor - (Name of a friend) I can discuss this with	I will get up at 6 AM daily and spend 1 hour in prayer and the Word. I will study God's Favor. I will write down what God shows me and share 2x/ month with friends.	_____ (Write a date that is 40 days from the start date).	Check when com- pleted. This creates account- ability and helps you measure results.
Emotional/ Soul Tasks: I will overcome frustration by con- fessing Scripture and stop- ping to pray when I feel frustrated. I will identify the root cause of my frustration to deal with the problem.	- Bible Concordance - Covenant Friends - Articles or other materials dealing with my root cause	I will confess 3 Scriptures 3 times per day over my emotions and will. I will call a friend when I get frustrated. I will keep a "Success Log" and record each time I overcome frustration.	_____ (Write a date that is 40 days from the start date).	

TASKS	POTENTIAL RESOURCES	STRATEGIC PLAN	COMPLETION DATE	✔
Physical Tasks: I will lose 10 pounds. I will work out 3 days per week and eat right.	- Gym - Friend to work out with	Create a monthly workout/ eating chart and write down what I accomplished.	———— (Write a date that is 40 days from the start date).	
Social Relation- ship Tasks: I will be more sensitive to my spouse. I will set aside one night each week for a date.	- Spouse - Friend to discuss ideas with - Book on marriage or relationships	I will listen to my spouse and spend quality time I will read and study with a view to changing ME, not him/her Schedule a date each week.	———— (Write a date that is 40 days from the start date).	
Financial Tasks: I will not buy on impulse or increase my credit card debt. I will give $___ as seed. I name my harvest ————. I will increase my knowledge on giving and stewardship.	- Biblical Concordance - Spouse or friends to call and discuss with - Books, CD's websites or articles to increase education	I will confess financial Scriptures daily. I will pray before I purchase anything and will only move when I have the peace of God and total agreement from my spouse. I will look for opportunities to sow I will study finances at least once each week.	———— (Write a date that is 40 days from the start date).	

Now you can create an Execution Goal Chart on your own, or you can use the one created for you in *The Focus Fulfilled Life Workbook*.

What to do at End

At the end of your 40 Days of Focus, you will review your Execution Goal Chart and create My Focus Results Chart that will capture your successes and achievements. In this final process, you will once again write in your objectives, but this time you will capture the final results. In addition to this, you will write down what you learned during the process that you can use in the future and take with you into your next 40 Day Focus.

The final stage in the process is to bring praise and thanksgiving back to God and thank Him for His faithfulness in providing the results you were standing on for the past 40 days. This chart captures the results and can also be used as a testimony to others who were standing in faith and prayer with you for the past 40 days. It is so important to testify what God has done for you. This will build your faith and inspire others. God will continue to show you favor and bring even more blessings to you. When my daughter was healed, I couldn't contain it — I had to share it with others. When I was called back three years after being downsized, you could not shut me up! I told everybody what God did for me. I had a testimony! This gave me the opportunity to share my faith with others. I was able to stay focused and believe God's Word and His promises came true. This one thing I know and can stand on — God will always do His part and bring about the manifestation.

In 1994, I was in a special service and I heard the Lord tell me to ask my boss for three specific things. First, that I would get a new position in the company as Senior Sales Representative. Second, that I would get a $10,000 raise since I was already selling and managing more volume than the current Senior Sales Representatives. And finally, to get a reduction in my territory responsibilities since I was managing an area that had too much for one person to handle. I heard God say to believe for it within the next 30 days! Now, what would you do? I heard the voice of the Lord. I was physically drained and stressed out managing all these people and this large territory. I went to my spiritual coverings (my pastor and my small group leader) and submitted what I heard to them to see if they agreed. Both felt a quickening and a peace that this was from God and told me to go for it. Now what? I prayed for boldness and that week, when I flew into the city where the office was located, I asked the Lord to prepare the way for me. That night, my boss and I were the only two left in the office. I went to him and laid down a piece of paper with all the facts on it, what I was currently doing for the company and my three requests. I asked him if it was possible for him to review this over the next 30 days. I left that night with great confidence that I had heard God. About three weeks later, I received a call from my boss. He told me that he reviewed my requests, that the company valued me as a loyal employee, AND that he would grant my requests in the 30 day time frame. What a God we serve!! Can you imagine how big my testimony got when I was able to share about how big our God is! I encourage you to write down and do not forget what the Lord has done for you. Rehearse your victories. Declare God's favor and tell others what God has done. I keep a log each year where I detail this out. This helps me to remember success so I can tell everyone I see – God is good! In times of struggle, this reminds me that God's promises are true and helps me to stand firm.

My Focused Results

Document and capture those objectives where you have seen the results you were seeking, standing on and praying

to God for in the past 40 days. Those objectives that are still not fully manifested should carry over to your next 40 day period of focus until you see the final results. It is okay to rest between. No one can remain in focused pursuit without rest. But remember, persistence is the key to victory! The Bible says in Proverbs 13:12, "*Hope deferred makes the heart sick, but when the desire (results) are fulfilled, it is a tree of life!*

Below is an example of a Focused Results Chart. Use this example to create your own chart, or refer to the Focus Fulfilled Life Workbook.

MY FOCUSED RESULTS!

OBJECTIVE	RESULTS	COMMENTS
Example: I will give $500 as seed in the next 40 Days.	Example: I gave $100 to my neighbor. (She came to church with me the following week!) I named my harvest "Salvation for my Family." I gave $250 to my church's building fund. I named my harvest "Pay Cash for a Home Repair." I gave $150 to my pastor and his wife. I named my harvest "New Contracts."	Example: I learned that God supplies seed. I was able to spend less money and therefore have more money to give during this season. After giving money to my neighbor, I had an open door to talk to my mother about Jesus! I was able to pay for fixing my roof without debt. I received two new contracts and saw increase on the job.

FOCUS Points

A SUMMARY OF WHAT YOU HAVE LEARNED

Chapter Eight Focus Points

- To execute your plan, you must remain focused on it daily.

- Make sure the tasks you develop in the Execution Goal Chart are ones you can do on a daily basis. They should be "bite-sized" and easy to execute.

- Be in faith and expectation that you will see major results.

- Be ready to testify about the goodness of God.

Chapter Nine

Let's Get STARTED!

Are you ready to have a focus fulfilled life? Then let's get started! I have created a workbook that will help you maintain this process on a daily basis. As a young teenager attending a Christian camp one summer, I was provided with a year-long Bible reading log. This simple tool helped me read the Word daily. After each day's reading, the workbook provided specific questions to help me reflect and review such as, "What does this mean to me?" and, "How do I apply this to my life today?" I have successfully used this process for many years and can testify how much it helped me focus on goals and achieve things that God has blessed me with during the past 30 years. I suggest you use *The Focus Fulfilled Life Workbook* to successfully capture and incorporate the process into your daily life. The workbook contains all the material you need to complete a 40 day cycle along with Scriptures already available to use pertaining to your particular objective and goals.

Getting Started

In this final chapter, I want to reintegrate the flow of this process.

- Identify and capture key learnings – What worked and what didn't work in your past successes and failures?

- Perform a Needs Assessment to prepare yourself before beginning your 40 Days of Focus. This step is important to determine, "What Do I Need to Focus On?"

- Identify objectives and goals based on the five key areas: Spiritual, Emotional/Soul, Physical, Social/ Relationships and Financial/Economic.

- Begin to gather and write down Scriptures pertaining to each of the five key areas. There are 40 Scriptures for each area provided for you in the Focus Fulfilled Life Workbook.

- Develop OGSM'S (Objectives, Goals, Strategies, Measures) in each of the five key areas using a Daily Focus Point for each Objective and Goal.

- Create an Execution Goal Chart focusing on tasks and strategies that are reasonable and manageable for you to complete on a daily basis.

- Capture your results using the My Focused Results chart and begin to testify about God's faithfulness.

- Celebrate, rest and prepare for the next 40 Days Of Focus

Focus Fulfilled Life
40 Day Small Group Focus

I encourage you to involve your church or organization in a specific 40 Days of Focus. This can be accomplished through small groups to help keep people focus on a defined, corporate objective to see greater results. Your church or organization can establish a leader to oversee these groups or incorporate this process into any small group program that currently exists. By using our 40 Days of Focus DVD Series and Workbook, establishing corporate OGSM's, and maintaining accountability, it is possible for a group of people to become focused on a goal or objective that will benefit your whole church or organization.

You can order your copy of
The Focus Fulfilled Life
DVD SERIES and *WORKBOOK*
by visiting
edturose.com

Personal Testimonies from Others

The Focus Fulfilled Life Seminar has been taught around the United States and many personal testimonies have been shared with me from people who began to focus on specific areas for 40 days and have seen tremendous results.

God Shows Up for Shelley's Son

Since I attended the Focus Fulfilled Life seminar, there are really cool things that the Father has going on for my family and me.

- God has completely redeemed the horrendous way that our son was treated by his basketball coach. Our son has been given the last open spot on a local Christian College basketball team.

- God has brought in 50% of our son's college tuition and He has promised to bring in the rest.

- Also, God has given me the opportunity to mentor a young couple who are new in their walk with the Lord.

(Shelly, Georgia)

Dan Is Debt Free!

When I began to focus on getting out of debt, I asked Ed Turose to stand with my wife and I for God to release us from a debt of $20,000. Ed's question to me was "What do you have in your hands that God can bless?" I owned about 20 acres of land and was led to sell some timber on about 10 acres of land. The first company offered me $5,000 for the timber on the 10 acres. I immediately called Ed and told him, but he said, "What are you believing for?" I replied, "$20,000!" Ed said, "This is not God. Wait!"

Now, I wanted to take the $5,000 and put it in the bank and believe for another $15,000, but there was no agreement to what Ed was asking me about believing for the entire $20,000. I refused the offer. About two months later another company called and told me they would give me $3,500 for the same timber. Now, I called Ed and told him we missed God! Ed said, "What are you believing God for?" I said, "$20,000" Ed said, "This is not God. Wait!"

About six months later, another company came and offered me almost five times as much for the same timber. Their offer was $23,000! I called Ed. He said, "This is God. Sell!" Then Ed told me that God was so good that He gave me the $20,000 to become debt free, $2,000 to give as a tithe to my local church and another $1,000 to sow as an offering to see another harvest. I am thankful I stayed focused on what I was believing God for and did not give in when I received the first offer. God is awesome and when you focus, He always does his part!

(Dan, Pennsylvania)

Joe's House Gets Sold

I am a contractor. I asked Ed Turose to pray with me to sell a particular house that my company built (valued at over $250,000) that had been on the market for over two years, but was not selling. Ed told me to stay focused on selling the house and continue speaking over the property daily that it was sold. About a week later, we met for prayer and Ed felt that there was a problem concerning the building of the house and a relationship that had gone bad. Taken aback, I proceeded to tell Ed that my brother and I built the house together but during the build we both became offended with each other and separated from working together. The house was the last project we had worked together on and it had been two years since the incident. Ed immediately told me to go to my brother and ask forgiveness for the offense and sow the opposite seed of love to him. I obeyed and did it that same day.

The following day I received a call from the realtor that the house was sold! My wife and I rejoiced! Not only did God release the sale of the house, but He restored the relationship between my brother and my family — an even greater blessing!

(Joe, Pennsylvania)

My Testimonies

Renovations Covered

I also was blessed because of Joe's house being sold. I was saving up for renovations to the bathrooms in my home at that time and had $1,000 in the bank set aside for this. The Lord spoke to me to sow that $1,000 to a friend of ours who just started a new ministry and then I named that seed to provide money or whatever way God wanted to move for the renovation. I needed at least $10,000 to fix up both bathrooms. After Joe sold the house, he called me, telling me that the Lord spoke to him and told him that whatever I was believing for, he was supposed to bless me with and provide what I needed. Needless to say, Joe and his crew provided for my wife and I, giving us new bathroom fixtures (high quality), new closets, and free labor to complete the work. The total cost of the project was over $12,000 and I received it free! Glory to God! Why? I became seed-minded to help this ministry and God met my need! Both financial needs that we were focusing on were met and a relational need was restored.

Generations Affected

I want to testify that you can sow into the next generation. You can plant seed and name harvest for your children and your children's children. From the time she was a small child, my wife and I taught our daughter,

Theresa, to focus on the Word of God and activate her faith to see results. Her life is a testimony of God's goodness flowing through to the next generation.

Once while watching a fictional movie called "That Thing You Do" (about a 50's band in Erie, Pennsylvania who write one song and become a "one hit wonder," only to allow their ego and other distractions to cause the group to disband), the Lord spoke to me. He told me that this is exactly what is happening to the family generations within the church. A mother and father get saved and begin to serve God, only to allow their children to become distracted in the world system and "wash out" of the church, producing a "one hit generation" for God! Where are the next generation, and the next who will serve God and be stronger and greater in their faith than our generation? Wow, that hit me so hard! I became determined to see generation after generation of my seed line be sold out to God. I began confessing that the generations in my line would be filled with God and fully

The generations in my seed line will serve God!

serve Him until Jesus returns! My job is to go as high as I can seeking the Lord, and then expect my seed line will go higher than me.

My daughter is married to a tremendous man of God, named Jaron. They are debt free living in a home that is completely paid for, they both work fulltime in high paying jobs, they sow into the church, both in offerings and by using their gifts in the church as leaders in worship, in children's church and in leadership training. They are being used by God in a mighty way. They are only in their mid-twenties and blessed beyond measure! Why? Because my wife and I refused to give in to the devil. We never expected that Theresa would be disobedient. It never came out of my mouth, and I would never believe the lie from Satan that my kids would rebel. Why would you believe that lie? It is time we stand and believe God that generation after generation will be committed to serve and glorify God until the day we leave planet earth!

Mother Healthy and Whole at 85 years Old

This testimony is about my mother who still works full time at 85 years old. I have always focused on our family line not dying from any disease or leaving the earth prematurely. I will not put up with the devil of disease, cancer or premature death affecting any of my loved ones. My mother was diagnosed with a small mass in her chest area. The doctors were saying it was probably cancer, but I knew better. Why? Because I have been confessing healing Scriptures over the life of my family for years and know God's Word is true concerning health and wholeness. I have had to get my mother to focus on the Word, even in her eighties. I would hear her complain of a few ailments and I would constantly remind her, "Mom, focus on the Word and confess healing Scriptures three times over your body every day."

One Monday, they took my mother in and operated on her, placing a scope down her chest to see if the mass was cancerous. A few hours later the doctor came back and said it was nothing — no cancer. Following the procedure, she was in a lot of pain and so we prayed for a quick recovery. My mother was released from the hospital on Tuesday and was back to work on Thursday! God is the Provider and the Healer. If we will stay focused on using His Word by confessing it and releasing our faith in expectation on a daily basis — into every area; spiritual, soul/personal, physical, social/relationships and financial/economic — He will prove Himself faithful and meet our every need.

God Redeems Me!

I have one final testimony I want to share with you of how the focus fulfilled lifestyle can produce greater results. I want to encourage your faith and motivate you to try the process and see how God will move!

God redeemed me from being fired from a Fortune 500 Company. I was a regional sales manager working for a major Fortune 500 Company and was on a yearly review with my new boss. I realized from the start that this new boss and I had some personality conflicts, yet I embraced his management style and determined to serve him in the same way that I did for my prior boss. I was in the yearly review, going through each of the management categories that I would be graded on, with a 5 being the highest mark you can get. Very few people would received a 5, and a 3 was considered a good mark (a 3 indicated that you were doing the job and doing it effectively). My former boss always graded me very high, giving me all 3's, 4's and even a few 5's based on my performance. However, this year was different. My new boss was a very task-oriented individual and had a tremendous gifting to manage projects and put processes in place. I was an out-of-the-box thinker, and that year I had finished as the number one regional manager in financial management and as the number two regional manager in achieving volume objectives. I was pleased with my performance, but my new boss told me that he did not like the *way* I did it. He gave me 3's on most of the performance criteria, but then gave me a zero and two 1's on my evaluation. I was totally shocked! He informed me that I was on 90 days probation and if I did not correct these areas, that I would be terminated.

I remember leaving the company headquarters, realizing I was in a battle for my seed sack (God is my Provider, my seed sack is God's conduit for providing seed to sow through my employment). As I flew back home I wrestled in my spirit. I said, "Lord, what is this?" He told me, "It is a battle and a test. How are you going to win this?"

My first thought was to reach out to the Vice President, a personal friend of mine and complain of the unfair treatment. The Lord quickly chided me and said, "Let Me redeem you!" It was then that I realized that I was going to have to fight and focus on this by going to work in the natural and by sowing specific Scriptures over this battle I was in. In the meantime, one of my peers was promoted. He was assigned to work with me to see where the problems were and to monitor if I was going to change or be terminated. He came to the market and flat out told me I was in trouble and that I was gone in 90 days if these areas were not corrected. I began to look for a Scripture to confess and the Lord showed me Isaiah 54:17, "*But no weapon that is formed against you shall prosper, and **every tongue that shall rise against you in judgment you shall show to be in the wrong**. This (peace, righteousness, security, triumph over opposition) is the heritage of the servants of the Lord.*"

I began to aggressively confess that I would show them to be in the wrong. When this peer came to me and began to review my processes already in place, he told me that two out of three areas were above average and he would have given me at least a 3 or 4 in each of these areas.

In the final area, he agreed that it was not completely up to a 3, but was not a zero. I focused my attention on both the natural and spiritual principles and after the 90 days, was given a complete sign of approval and was not terminated. However, God still was not finished with the process. The probationary period ended in June of that year. I finished with another successful year of God blessing me in my business by focusing on His voice, the voice behind His Word, and obeying it. I continued to guard my heart, making sure I did not hold any grudges, but instead supporting and serving my boss. In March of the next year, we had our annual national sales meeting to review the successes from the prior year's business. That year they were honoring the best Manager and Food Brokers in the country. They only name three (one in each area of the country). They called out the best Manager and Food Broker in the East and guess what? They called my name! Now, I had been on probation for 90 days during that year, and yet God redeemed me and honored me with national recognition. My counter part (who manages the Food Broker side) was also called up. He looked over to me and said, "How did we get here?" I said, "God has redeemed me and I give Him praise!"

You see, I could have gone to the Vice President or tried to work it out on my own. Instead I began to focus on what God told me — that He would redeem me. I focused on the Word of God and began confessing Isaiah 54:17. Would you not agree that God was able to show every tongue that rose against me to be in the wrong! This is just one more fantastic reason why you can't shut me up... I HAVE to testify about the goodness of God! Are you ready to trust God? Are you ready to focus and see successful results?

"For the eyes of the Lord run to and fro throughout the whole earth to show Himself strong on behalf of those whose hearts are perfect toward Him."

2 Chronicles 16:9 NKJV

Next Steps

I want to encourage you that this process of a focus fulfilled life can take you to the next level of seeing greater results than you have experienced in the past. It is my confession and I continually say, "The Word of God works for me!" God is not a respecter of persons, but He **IS** looking for those individuals who will draw nigh to Him so He can draw nigh to them and empower them to prosper so that we can be a blessing on every occasion (James 4:8, Genesis 12:2-3).

Prayer
Please confess this prayer.

Father, I thank you for your faithfulness. I ask that You help me begin to focus on those areas where I need help. I ask for the Holy Spirit to come and teach me the Word of God and help me to hear Your voice every day. I need the ability to stay with this process and see the greater results. Satan, I bind you over my life and I take authority over you, rebuking you and commanding that you remove your hands from me and my family. I am a child of the Most High God and I call upon God now to help me establish a focus fulfilled lifestyle and to have a new, fresh mental and spiritual attitude. I ask you, Lord, to show me the best objectives, goals and strategies I need to execute on a daily basis to see a greater level of success. I now thank You for helping me and I give You all the glory and praise for what You are about to do in my life. I will go to the next level and I will testify about Your goodness. Amen.

Appendix

The POWER of FOCUS
Takes Your BUSINESS
to the NEXT LEVEL

Workplace and Organizational Focus

The principles found in *The Focus Fulfilled Life* also apply to businesses, ministries, and organizations. If you are ready to take your organization to the next level, the power of focus can help!

Victory Corporate Consulting (VCC) was created to help businesses, organizations and ministries achieve their goals and reach their destinies through strategic marketplace or ministry solutions.

Recent statistics reveal the following:

- 85% of businesses or organizations do not have a vision or a plan to achieve their purpose and mission.

- Out of the 15% who do, **only 5%** are actively planning their work and working their plan for the vision to be successful.

VCC is a full service consulting, training and resource company focused on increasing *profitability*, growing *productivity*, gaining *efficiencies* and helping you save *time* and *money* by offering the following strategic business solutions:

- We provide Strategic Planning and Follow-Through Strategies

- We help you develop the ICES model. (Innovation/Concepts/Execution/Solutions)

- We provide Executive Leadership Training

- We provide Executive Team Building Training

- We initiate effective Sales and Marketing Strategies

- We implement Position Match (Hiring and Job Requirement Positioning)

This process has proven successful for business after business. You already possess the raw materials — let us help you master your strengths, overcome your weaknesses and step into a new dimension of growth and opportunity! Our process includes the following:

⊶ PERSONAL

- You will receive a thorough personal review of your company or organization's strengths, motivations and behavioral styles that can help you become more efficient and effective in your management style.

⊶ PROCESS

- You will be able to identify key learning's from past experiences and create processes to increase profitability and productivity within your business or organization.

⊶ PLANNING

- We will help you develop and create excellence through a proven strategic planning model that is focused on achieving your objectives and goals with proven follow through strategies.

⊶ PERSONNEL

- The Position Match Program will save you time and money. It will help you hire the best possible candidate for a new position. This process will also help place current employees in roles and functions that produce greater results.

⌛ PEFORMANCE

- Our training focuses on improving performance through executive leadership, team and sales programs that will increase productivity and gain efficiencies within your business or organization.

VCC will work with you and key individuals within your organization to develop a strategic business plan that will help you execute and identify the proper follow-through strategies to meet your objectives. At the end of this planning process, your business or organization will be totally focused on achieving the results you have desired for years.

With over 55 combined years of Fortune 500 and administrative experience, both Jim Sanderbeck and Ed Turose, operators of Victory Corporate Consulting, offer their expertise to help businesses, organizations and ministries achieve their goals and plan for the future. To learn more or receive a free Needs Assessment for your organization, visit edturose.com and click on VCC.

STRATEGIC MINISTRY AND MARKETPLACE SOLUTIONS TRAINING MODULES

PLANNING MODULES	FOCUS AREA	PROCESS
Executive Leadership I	Behavioral & Motivational Outcomes - Understanding Self	DISC Computer Program and Training
Executive Leadership II	Enhancing Communication	DISC Understanding Blending
Executive Team Building	Understanding Self	Team Building Profile - Five Core Values

Executive Values Training	Understanding Value Styles	Value Style Profile
Position Match I	Position People in the Right Place	Profile
Position Match II	Hire Right the First Time	Profile
Stress Management	Reduce stress	Stress Management Profile
Business Keys to Succeed	ICES	Innovation, Concepts, Execution and Solutions
Strategic Business Planning I	Creating a Strategic Plan	14 Key Management Areas
Strategic Business Planning II	Creating OGSM's and Goal Chart	OGSM and Goal Charts
A Winning Start – *by Tim Turose*	New Business Start-ups	www.awinningstart.com

www.edturose.com

FOCUS

Package

Your journey to see greater results begins
with the Focus Fulfilled Life Progression!

- Identify Goals in your Spiritual, Emotional, Physical, Social and Financial Life
- Gather and Meditate on Specific Scriptures related to these Goals
- Develop Daily Strategies and Capture your Results
- Celebrate, Rest and Testify of God's Goodness and Faithfulness!

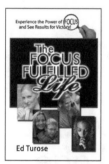

The Focus Fulfilled Life
Book - 160 pages

Discover what life would be like if you were able
to focus on a goal and see greater results. This
book will begin the journey for your success!

The Focus Fulfilled Life
DVD SERIES

Ed Turose lays out the process for
40 Days of Focus in this powerful
DVD.

The Focus Fulfilled Life
WORKBOOK

Put the process into practice and
make it work for you! This workbook
contains key scriptures, faith confessions,
daily journal, progress charts and more!
The workbook covers each of the five
key areas of focus: spiritual, physical
emotional, social and financial.

Get the tools you need to take your business to the next level!

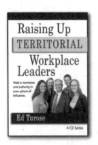

into a new dimension of growth and opportunity!

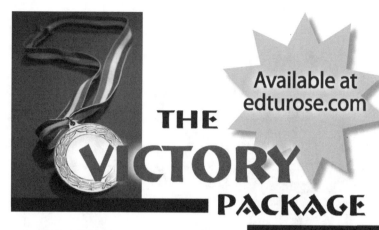

 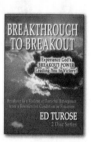
 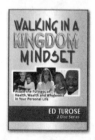

ED TUROSE

Utilizing the anointing of exhortation and empowerment, Ed Turose has a gifting that bridges the gap between the workplace and ministry. Ed has an anointing to release finances and empower people to go to the next level and to fulfill the covenant of Genesis 12:2-3 that we are be blessed to be a blessing.

Ed Turose has 30 years of business experience as a strategic planner and financial manager for two of the most prestigious Fortune 500 Companies, the Coca-Cola Company and UniLever, the largest consumer packaged goods company in the world.

He is the developer of "Ministers of Kingdom Finance," "Marketplace Empowerment," and "Youth Empowerment" that helps equip and mentor individuals to impact the marketplace and become financially empowered to build the Kingdom of God. He has helped facilitate organizations, churches, and businesses to strategically achieve their goals.

Since 1996, Ed has been the President of Victory Corporate Consulting, a full service, on-site consulting, training and resource company focused on taking businesses and organizations to a higher level by increasing productivity, growing profitability and gaining efficiencies. He is an expert in strategic planning, executive leadership, team building training, sales and marketing strategies, hiring, and creating new ideas through his ICES model in Innovation, Concepts, Execution and Solutions.

He has produced two intensive training seminars called "Business Keys to Succeed" and "The Business Anointing." He has traveled and spoken with Apostle John Kelly in the WealthBuilder Marketplace Seminars. He is a member of ICA (International Coalition of Apostles), an elder and worship leader in his local church and a certified trainer in both the DISC Behavioral Personality System and CIBN (Christian International Business Network).

Ed Turose is available for the following speaking and empowerment opportunities:

☛ Focus Fulfilled Life Seminars

- Ed will come to your church, ministry, business or organization and provide wisdom and insight to help your members or employees get focused to gain better results. Ed is available for local or national speaking engagements to groups of all sizes.

☛ Speaking Engagements

- Ed offers an anointed financial breakthrough ministry to both the local church and the marketplace.

☛ Marketplace Empowerment Seminars

- A seminar focused on business and spiritual keys to succeed.

☛ Youth Empowerment Seminars

- Ed empowers youth to take their place in the Kingdom at a young age.

☛ Consulting/Coaching

- Ed can take you and your business, ministry or organization to the next level!

To learn more, to purchase resources, or to schedule Ed for a seminar or event, visit edturose.com today!